The author, on Loch Maree

PAVILIONS BY THE SEA

Tom Laughton

PAVILIONS BY THE SEA

The Memoirs of an Hotel-Keeper

ROBIN CLARK

First published in Great Britain 1977 by
Chatto & Windus Ltd
Second impression 1977
Third impression 1977
This edition published 1978 by Robin Clark Ltd
15 Leyden Road, Stevenage, Herts, SG1 2BW

© Tom Laughton 1977

Made and printed in Great Britain by
M C Print Co., Ltd., Stevenage, Herts.

ISBN 0 86072 015 2

CONTENTS

ILLUSTRATIONS

FOREWORD

Pavilions by the Sea is, as far as I know, the first book to describe the real inner life of a great hotel. Arnold Bennett was an assiduous collector of facts who spoilt them with fiction, — an outsider's view: Fothergill wrote amusingly about a country inn. Here we have the creative adventure of hotel keeping.

I must declare my personal interest in this book. Tom Laughton is a friend of mine. I share his love for the old town of Antibes, though he knows its corners and characters far better than I do, and I have listened many times to his analytical study of a certain small butcher in the rue de Sade, and his method of cutting a veal kidney. "This", I thought, "is the great hotelier saluting another artist of the good life." Rashly on one of these occasions I encouraged him to write a book, rashly because the hackneyed phrase "everyone has one book inside him" is deceptive and totally untrue. Everyone has the material in his memories for many books, but that's not the same thing at all.

> "Between the idea
> And the reality
> Between the motion
> And the act
> Falls the Shadow."

I hope he will forgive me for disclosing some details of this book's history. When I saw the first draft I was worried — the beginning was finely rendered, his family started alive from the page, his apprenticeship to farming was the best such account since Adrian Bell's *Corduroy*, a book which nearly turned me into a countryman, but. . .

but. . . I tried to wrap my criticisms up like a gift package but Laughton without hesitation untied the tinsel string. When after two years had passed I read the third draft of his book, I began to realise I was not dealing with an amateur but a professional. To an amateur his words are Holy Writ — the professional knows how far they will always fall short of what he wants to say. I became used to the letters from Yorkshire written to the signature tune, "I think I see what's wrong. I have started again." To what an inferno, I thought, has my unthinking encouragement condemned him. Why should a man who loves good painting, good wine and good food, living in a happy and well-deserved retirement, suffer in the evening of life what all writers must suffer — in Masefield's phrase "The long despair of doing nothing well"?

I am glad now to have been the judge who condemned him. The first paragraph of his book has the proud, confident, professional ring which the book never loses.

GRAHAM GREENE

AUTHOR'S PREFACE

This is a story about a family of hotel-keepers, one of whom became a world-famous actor. It was Graham Greene who suggested that I should write it, but when he did, he omitted to warn me how difficult it would be. "Write as you talk", he said, surprising advice from such a master-craftsman. As I struggled to follow his counsel, I came to realise my inadequacy. In the early stages I said to Graham, "It is going to take me a year!" "A year!" he replied. "My last book took me three years." So I plodded on. An eminent publisher suggested that I should enlist the services of a ghost writer. Crestfallen I again consulted Graham. He would have none of it, "You must write it all yourself", he said. The outcome has been that it has taken me over three years.

It is to my wife Isobel that I owe the greatest debt of gratitude. She has borne the brunt of my literary struggles. I am grateful for her encouragement and for her loving patience and understanding. I am also grateful for her help with my grammar, her knowledge of the subject is better than mine.

My literary friend Tom Bentley has helped me throughout with his interest and encouragement. He assisted me with the preparation of my manuscript for the publishers. It was he who suggested the title. He has been a true friend and I am deeply grateful.

Finally I must thank Grahame Martin-Turner, who introduced me to my publishers and also Ian Parsons whose expert editing and advice has helped me to produce the final typescript.

To my wife

ISOBEL

who has coped so lovingly
with a burnt out hotel-keeper
and brought him to life again.

CHAPTER I

A FAMILY OF HOTEL-KEEPERS

My father returning from a day's shooting, found mother
serving in the vaults bar at the Victoria hotel. He called her
out into the little hotel office and quietly told her that he
hadn't married her to serve behind the bar. "No", replied
mother, "neither did I marry you to go bankrupt", and
returned to her work in the bar. She was carrying my
younger brother Frank at the time.

Mother had good reason to take her work seriously, as
she had been brought up in a public house at Seaham Harbour and had lived through her father's bankruptcy. The
experience had bitten deeply and she was determined that
this should never happen to her own family. Father had not
the same drive; farm bred he remained a countryman at
heart. All his life he spent what time he could in the open
air, going to his garden, and as often as possible he would
leave the hotel, in summer to fish and in winter to shoot.
With mother it was different; her family and the business
came first. She had no outside interests other than her
religion; she was a Catholic and was bringing her children
up in the Catholic faith.

The Victoria was a small hotel catering mainly for commercial travellers, it had three public bars, of which the
"vaults", catering mostly for workmen, was the busiest. It
is situated immediately opposite to the entrance of the
Scarborough railway station. Running it was well within
their capabilities. My parents had gone there, as managers,
when they were first married, starting on a joint salary of
thirty shillings per week. On mother's initiative they gave
up being the managers and took over the hotel as tenants

so that the business became their own. They made the Victoria into the best commercial hotel in the town, mother running the accommodation side and father doing the catering and looking after the cellars and bars.

They had three children, all boys — Charles the eldest, myself, Tom and my younger brother Frank. There was four years' difference between each of our ages. We were all born at the Victoria, Frank the youngest was born just a year before the family moved from the Victoria across to the Pavilion, a larger and more substantial hotel in a better position but only one hundred and fifty yards away.

At the Victoria, our day nursery was on the first floor at the front of the hotel overlooking the railway station entrance, the night nursery was at the back of the hotel on an upper floor overlooking the stables. We did not see a great deal of our parents, father was out most of the day and mother was too busy in the hotel. But we were never short of company as we were a great attraction to the hotel staff. Of these the one whom I remember was Hepsebiah Thompson, the book-keeper receptionist; she had a deep, rich, creamy voice, fine eyes and dark hair. What a voice! It must have been a great attraction to the customers. If I knew of such another voice in any hotel today, I should make a special journey for the sole pleasure of being welcomed by it. She was the most memorable, but we had many other friends amongst the staff, who would call into the nursery to join in our games.

Mother, a great believer in fresh air, encouraged our nanny to take us out as much as possible. Once clear of the hotel, we never progressed in the normal manner; we either chuffed chuffed away with bent arms working like railway steam engine connecting rods or energetically bowled hoops along the pavements.

We were usually taken inland up the town to Falsgrave Park, where we would launch our hoops down the precipitous slopes or play in a derelict bandstand, which seemed to us to have been left there especially for our benefit.

Our favourite way was up the road at the back of the station, where through the tall railings we could watch the trains puffing smoke and blowing steam. The greatest treat of all was to see a train pull out, the train belching smoke with a frantic scrabbling of the wheels, then as the train moved sedately off, slowly gathering speed, hear the lovely chuff, chuff, chuff and finally a triumphant whistle as the train was gradually lost to view.

In one of the two snug bars at the entrance to the hotel, there was a black ram's head with massive curling horns and a silver snuffbox mounted in the skull. Father would take a pinch of snuff, lay it along the back of his clenched fist and invite us to take a sniff, always with cataclysmic results. I preferred to stroke the ram's broad Roman nose — it must have been a magnificent animal.

Sometimes when we left the hotel we would set our course for the sands; two little boys in sailor suits, equipped with buckets, spades and shrimping nets. Through the station yard with the horse drawn waggonettes and the sweet smell of horse dung, down the valley and along the valley road to the sea; passing a line of one-horse phaetons drawn by horses driven by postillions dressed in faded jockey costumes; on to the sands and along the sands below the walls of the Spa promenade, to our destination, The Children's Corner, the place where the so-called "best children" played. In those days Scarborough was a very class conscious town. "The best people" resided on the South Cliff, tradesmen and shopkeepers lived and worked in the centre of the town, the lodgings and boarding houses were mostly on the North Side.

On the front the divisions were marked by the Spa, the exclusive resort of the prosperous and respectable with a sprinkling of the aristocracy; in the centre the foreshore where the cheap restaurants and fun palaces catered for the day trippers; and the final barrier of the Castle Hill between the South Bay and the North Bay which catered mainly for the boarding house trade.

Presumably we were taken to The Children's Corner south of the Spa so that we could mix with our betters. If the tide came in when we were at The Children's Corner the only way back was over the Spa; the usual entrance fee to the Spa was sixpence but children trapped by the tide were allowed over on payment of a penny toll. It was an ordeal passing over the Spa, past the bandstand and through the well dressed throng, where scruffy children with buckets and spades were clearly out of place. But there was a treat in store at the north end of our passage across the Spa. Here we could look down and enjoy Catlin's Pierrots performing on their small canvas-covered stage set upon the sands immediately below. Will Catlin, the leader of the troupe, was a hero to Charles; someone larger than life, flamboyant, full of infectious energy. The Pierrots were dressed in voluminous white jackets and trousers, decorated with large black bobbles and wearing a white pointed felt hat adorned with a black bobble on the side. We could never see enough of them, especially Charles, who gave imitations of Will Catlin singing his favourite song — "Here comes the galloping Major". It was probably Will Catlin who first infected Charles with the theatre bug.

We were not often taken out by mother, except on Sundays when she took us to early Mass at the Roman Catholic Church.

The highlight of the social week in Scarborough was the Sunday church parade on the South Cliff promenade. The well dressed congregations emerged from the fashionable churches after the eleven o'clock services and congregated on the Esplanade, all walking sedately to display their finery. It was the only occasion on which father and mother would take us out together. We would cross the penny toll bridge over the valley to join the awesomely respectable throng. Charles used to tell the story how on one of these occasions he noticed a particularly well dressed and attractive young woman. Pulling mother's hand he excitedly pointed to her saying "Look mother, look at the pretty lady!" Mother gave one quick glance — "Hush Charlie — look the other way, she's not a lady, she's an actress".

The fact that we attended the church parade was an indication that we were going up in the world. The Victoria was regarded as the best commercial hotel in the town, but mother was not satisfied. Her eyes turned to the hub of Scarborough, where stood the more impressive Pavilion Hotel, three times the size of ours. Despite its superior situation it was doing badly; so badly indeed, that it came on the market. Mother urged father to buy it, but quite happy at the Victoria he was reluctant to incur the heavy debt that our purchase of the Pavilion would involve. Mother's ambition and determination won the day. The bank refused to lend us the money, but eventually Uncle George, a Sheffield steel manufacturer married to mother's younger sister, stepped in and financed the purchase. So in 1908 we moved from the Victoria across to the Pavilion.

I do not remember anything of the move, being only five years old at the time. There would not be a great deal of change for us children, for all our friends amongst the staff came with us, including Hepsebiah Thompson. With us came all our regular customers; it was vital that they should. The purchase of the hotel had been a desperate gamble; there were no resources to tide us over bad times, immediate success was essential if the business was to survive.

Oblivious of our precarious situation, it was a delightful change for us children and we enjoyed exploring every corner of our new home. Our quarters were tucked away at the far end of the first floor wing, the day nursery looking over the main street and the night nursery looking over the back of the hotel. Now there were four floors of bedrooms to explore, each with a chambermaid's pantry and these, providing the chambermaid was one of our friends, were amongst our favourite hide-outs.

We liked the basement best of all, with the kitchens, larders, wine and beer cellars, provision stores and boiler house. Our ally Chef Weiser ruled the kitchen; my own special friend was Albert Midgeley, the cellarman. We penetrated to the basement whenever we could. Once through the service doors at the head of the basement steps, we were in a different world, where people were more themselves, talking, laughing, even shouting. Arthur Drysdale, the head porter, quiet almost servile in the hall of the hotel, was a different man on the staff side of the service door. Then there were the delivery men. One I could never forget, Watercress Jim, a wild looking character with wavy ginger hair and ginger whiskers (very like Charles when he played the beachcomber in "Vessel of Wrath"). He was cross-eyed but his voice was unexpectedly educated. He made his living by gathering watercress from streams around Ganton, a nearby village. He came trudging into Scarborough twice a week, with panniers over his shoulders packed with watercress, which he delivered to his customers. In the dark cellar passage, the dim light shining through his ginger locks, he was a sight worth seeing. It was said that he had been at Eton and had been decorated for bravery in the Boer War. He was certainly well educated and an impressive character.

We were always looking for people who would allow us to lend a hand — helping Albert to stick the labels on the bottled beer, feeding the corks into the hopper of the hand-operated bottle-corking machine, helping chef to feed his pet hedgehog (it lived under the sinks in the pan wash), helping the linen keeper to count the items of dirty linen and helping Winnie the second floor chambermaid to fill the hot water cans. Winnie was one of our favourites, a delightful young woman like a little hen robin. Filling hot water cans was a constantly recurring task in those days, as there was no running water in the bedrooms. All the water had to be carried in to the wash basins standing on marble-topped wash-stands. The chambermaid brought the hot water into the bedroom, lifted the jug of cold water out of the basin on to the floor and replaced it with an enamelled jug of hot water, draping a towel over it to keep it warm. Coal fires in the bedrooms were a commonplace. The customers even bathed in their bedrooms in hip baths carried in and placed before the fire, all the water for the bath having to be brought in.

The chambermaids had a frantically busy time, making the beds, cleaning the rooms, carrying coal from their pantry to the bedroom coal scuttles, carrying hot and cold water and answering bells for service; and in those days the bells were constantly ringing. But despite all this most of them were pleased to see us.

An hotel is more than just a building, it is a co-operative human effort. At the Pavilion, the guest was met on the station platform by Bob Moore our station porter, received at the reception desk by Miss Thompson with her beautiful creamy voice, taken up in the lift by Arthur Drysdale the hall porter, looked after in the bedroom by Winnie Harrington or one of the other chambermaids, seated in the dining room by Heseltine the head waiter, served by such waitresses as Norah Lishman or Edith Grant in their old fashioned broad-bibbed, wide-aproned uniforms, and after the meal served coffee by Driscoll the lounge waiter. In addition there were the staff behind the scenes, Chef Weiser and his kitchen brigade, Albert the cellarman, Vera the still room maid and many others. With so many staff to provide for it was fortunate that we had our regular commercial traveller customers from the Victoria to depend on. Not only for their custom, they helped to spread the name of the Pavilion throughout the North of England. Gradually the character of our business changed, we were no longer catering almost entirely for commercial travellers, we were attracting customers from a much wider field, including the county aristocrats.

Sir Tatton Sykes of Sledmere Hall, dressed in clothes that marked him as a man of country pursuits, became a regular winter customer. On arrival he would strip off up to half a dozen top coats. There is a story that he once sank down on the Pavilion steps mumbling, "My God, I'm paralysed", his trouble was that he had put on just one overcoat more than he could carry.

Amongst the guests that I recall were Sir George and Lady Ida Sitwell. It was their practice to stay at the Pavilion prior to taking up residence in their large house in the Scarborough Crescent. Sir George was tall and distinguished, Lady Ida extremely beautiful; together they made a fine patrician picture and their presence bestowed a feeling of regal patronage, not only on us but also on our staff and other guests. The Sitwells stayed with us for many years. Osbert stayed at the Pavilion, when he stood for Parliament as a Liberal candidate in the local constituency. His exquisite manners charmed everyone in the hotel. He was not elected, but if he had been, I doubt whether he would have been at home in the House of Commons.

The most lasting and important change in our clientele came from quite another direction. We began to attract customers from the West Riding of Yorkshire, substantial down to earth folk, who knew just what they wanted, good food, good service and good value; they got them at the Pavilion. Mother was responsible for the service and father for the food. At the front of the house mother became extremely well known and well respected; father was never so much in the public eye but the food he provided was the principal cause of our growing success.

The excellence of the food was mainly due to his expert marketing, which obtained for the kitchens all the best local produce. Every morning he set off from the hotel at six-thirty as the shop shutters were being taken down, to make sure that he had the first choice from what the tradesmen had to offer.

One of our greatest treats was when he took either Charles or myself with him; he would never take both of us, only one or the other.

At the butchers he would run his eyes over the sides of beef, carefully selecting the ones from which the sirloins and steak pieces were to be cut; looking for the creamy flecks of fat in the lean which give a marbled effect and are the sign of a well matured carcase. He would then turn to the carcases of lamb and the sides of pork, he selected only prime well fed meat. From the butchers he went on to the greengrocers. A gardener himself, he could judge at a glance the quality of what was being offered. The last call was down on the harbour fish quay, where fresh landed fish were laid out in orderly, shining, slimy rows; rank after rank of cod, haddock, whiting, woof, monkfish, lemon soles, plaice and dover soles, occasional turbot and halibut and sometimes even a lordly sturgeon. Everything was stiff fresh, except for the lobsters and crabs, which were still alive and struggling.

One day returned from shopping, we were in the larder talking to the chef. Father had bought an exceptionally large turbot, which was lying on the table in the centre of the room, having just arrived from the quayside. The fish was still alive, for with a frantic flap it fell with a crash on to the larder floor; for me it was a terrifying experience.

Mother still believed in fresh air and her recipe for a healthy life included a daily walk. Charles, on the other hand, hated walks; his passion was for entertainments, matinées at the cinema, Catlin's Pierrots and, his greatest favourites, the Fol-de-Rols performing at the Floral Hall. He developed a technique to satisfy both mother and himself. He would rush down to the foreshore, put one foot on the sands, a foot on the end of the harbour and a foot on the entrance to the Marine Drive and then make tracks to his chosen entertainment. Back at home the account of his walk was graphic and impressive, naturally there was no mention of the cinema or theatre. It kept mother happy and added the spice of forbidden fruit to his pleasure.

We lived in two worlds: the front of the hotel, where visitors and staff, and even us children, were expected to be on our best behaviour; the other world behind the service doors frequented by staff and tradesmen, where our friends made us welcome, where there always seemed to be something happening and where we learned to appreciate how many different sorts of people are required to make an hotel function. It taught us to appreciate the importance of even the lowliest member of the staff. As children we were more at home with panmen, kitchen porters and chambermaids than with the head Chef, and the Head Porter and the like. I have never lost my appreciation of the backroom men and women who are the foundation of every hotel organisation. Many of the staff at the Pavilion were with us throughout their working lives.

I once met one of our regular Pavilion customers coming out of a huge New York Hotel. He asked me what I thought of the American Hotels. I was staying at the Waldorf Astoria and I told him that in many respects I found them impressive. "Do you?" he replied. "I don't, I can't get service; everything for my room has to be ordered over the telephone and nothing arrives as ordered. Now take the Pavilion, all I have to do there is to press the bell, they know by experience what I want and it is brought before I order it. That's what I call service".

There was truth in his argument. New York was giving us an example of the shape of hotels to come, not only in America but all over the world. The bigger they get, the more impersonal the service and the less pleasure they afford.

CHAPTER II

AWAY TO SCHOOL

Not long after the move to the Pavilion I had my first experience of school, at Wheater's Academy in Albemarle Crescent, nor far from the hotel. Charles would take me by the hand, lead me across the main street up a back lane to the school yard. It was a wretched school conducted by Mr. Wheater with a single assistant and a drill sergeant. Mr. Wheater was a dapper little man with staring eyes and an upturned moustache, he taught with a cane in his hand. One day he seized Charles by the collar and flogged him in front of us all. I was horrified; it upset me far more than Charles, so much so that I refused to go back. When father discovered the reason, we were withdrawn from Wheater's and stayed at home until another school was found – Mr. Paton's in Princess Royal Terrace on the South Cliff. A much kinder school, where there were girls as well as boys and a fox terrier that girated madly to catch its own tail. For us it had one great advantage: to get there we had to cross the penny toll bridge which connected the centre of the town with the South Cliff. Usually we were able to save the penny by dashing down the valley and up the other side, our pennies clutched in our hands to be spent in Mrs. Linn's sweet shop in Ramshill Road, coconut cubes at a halfpenny an ounce, and my first real extravagance, a chocolate walnut whirl at two pence.

Charles was not at Paton's very long, he outgrew the school and moved to Scarborough College for a term. By this time the success of our Pavilion venture seemed assured, so much so that mother decided we should be sent to a Roman Catholic public school.

The school she chose was Beaumont College in the Thames Valley, run by Jesuits. The reason for the choice was that it was intended that Charles should be entered for a commission in the Royal Navy and Beaumont had a good record for successful naval entrants. However, Charles failed his first entrance examination, after which we were taken away from Beaumont and sent to another Jesuit public school, Stonyhurst College, situated on the slopes of the Lancashire fells, which was more convenient for Scarborough. Charles was sent direct to the college and I was sent to Hodder Place, which was the preparatory school for the college, and only two miles away from the main school.

At home religion had meant saying our morning and evening prayers and going to Church with mother every Sunday — that is as far as it went. Until we arrived at Stonyhurst religion had been rather a meaningless routine. At Hodder Place I came across a deeper meaning for the first time. The Jesuit colleges in England are a part of the public school system, except that the basic motive behind them is that the Jesuit education should be a foundation for the continuing growth and the strengthening of the Roman Catholic faith. The Jesuits are a most important body in Roman Catholic propaganda and at Stonyhurst the propaganda was constant both in teaching and by example. At Hodder there was a community of about six Jesuit teachers and at Stonyhurst College over sixty Jesuit priests and postulants, with a seminary for young men training for the priesthood close at hand.

Hodder Place was situated close to the river Hodder on a hillside above Paradise Valley. It accommodated about sixty little boys from seven to eleven years of age. In my time the Superior was a Father Cassidy of the Society of Jesus; he was a kindly man, the boys all liked him and none of us feared him. He never took classes, his principal duty seemed to be to give religious instruction, which he did by telling us simple stories of Jesus Christ and stories of the saints. He did it supremely well, one of his stories was of an uneducated lay brother, a sort of domestic monk who before he had joined the monastery had been a juggler. He had a devotion to the Blessed Virgin and when he wished to pray to her, he would go to the Lady Chapel and, bringing out his gear, he would silently juggle in front of her image. Years later I discovered where he had got it from; it was a story by Anatole France.

Father Cassidy was a great believer in the power of prayer. I drank it all in, in fact I became a little drunk. I can remember at about nine years of age praying before a Crucifix with my arms outstretched.

There was one episode that I recall with discomfort; I was competing in a billiard competition that I passionately wanted to win. I prayed that I might win it and promised that if God would help me to win I would try to convert father to our faith. I did win and in fulfilment of my obligation I sent father by post a penny Roman Catholic Catechism. I was not there to see him open the package, and he discreetly forbore to make enquiries as to why he had received the mysterious booklet.

If I had to leave home I don't think I could have been at a better place than Hodder to get over the shock. It was not all roses, the boys discovered that my parents were hotel-keepers, which was considered to be a very low occupation and I was made to feel it. The class system was rigidly applied in public schools, and Stonyhurst was no exception. The snobbery seemed to permeate not only the boys but even the Jesuit community. Boys from aristocratic families like the "De Traffords", the "Trappes-Lomaxes", the "Merry Del Vals" were recognised as having a special status.

Stonyhurst owed its establishment to the Welds, one of the aristocratic English families that had remained true to the Catholic faith. The Welds had acquired Stonyhurst about the year 1750; it had been the family seat of the Shireburn family. In 1794 the Welds gave Stonyhurst to the Jesuits. The aristocratic origin of the college seemed to have affected the attitude of the Jesuit community, who clearly regarded themselves as a part of the Roman Catholic aristocracy. This had the advantage that their standards were high, but there was a clash between their Christian teachings and the material attitude of the priests when they were in contact with the outside world. This was not noticeable at Hodder, where Father Cassidy was an example of Christian charity and humility.

Life at the college was very different from life at Hodder Place. Discipline at Stonyhurst was strict and it was enforced by a system of punishment administered by three priests known as the prefects. The headquarters of the prefects was in the college Armoury. The prefects superintended the recreation time, kept general order and carried out any punishments imposed in the classrooms. When a punishment was imposed, the boy had to report to the Armoury at a specified time, give his sentence to the prefect, who took him by the wrist, opened out the palm of his hand flat and dealt him six, eight or twelve strokes with the Ferula. The Ferula was an ingenious instrument about twenty-four inches long and two inches wide, probably made of leather and whalebone. Whatever it was made of, it was extremely painful. I believe it is an instrument peculiar to the Society of Jesus – an example of the Jesuits' ingenuity, and possibly a by-product of their activities within the Spanish Inquisition.

The mental discipline was as effective as the physical, the Jesuits never forgot their basic aim – the propagation of the Faith. At Hodder, Father Cassidy's talks and instructions were tremendously effective; at the College the religious teaching was put over with a sterner accent. Each year the climax of the year's religious teaching consisted of a three-day spiritual retreat. During the three days all normal activities ceased. All but the youngest boys had to keep silence for the whole period. Only spiritual books were allowed, all the boys having to attend a series of instructions and sermons lasting three whole days, which were given in the B●ys' Chapel by a highly skilled hot gospeller.

The first day of the retreat was usually devoted to the retreat director gaining the confidence of the boys by amusing and relaxing addresses. He gradually turned to more serious subjects, leading on to the horror of sin, from there to the utter despair of eternal damnation and lastly to the ineffable reward of eternal beatitude in heaven. It was the middle bit, the description of eternal damnation and the vivid attempt to describe eternal punishment that did the damage. "If one grain of sand was transported every thousand years until all the deserts of the world had been emptied, you would be no nearer to the end of eternal damnation". It was a wicked business.

I resisted it fairly well. During one retreat, my spiritual reading consisted of the novel "Five Nights", by Victoria Cross, sedately concealed in the hard back cover of "The Imitation of Christ"; but the retreats got me in the end. At the age of fourteen or fifteen I was in a vulnerable state, going through the usual masturbation period – instinctively feeling it was wrong but unsuccessfully trying to break myself of the habit. I was in a state prepared to accept that it was a deadly sin. Feeling that way, I listened with attention to the ominous words of the prophet of doom. I persuaded myself that after masturbating I was in danger of hell fire. For an extended period I was rushing to the confessional to purge myself of my daily sin and to save myself from the fires of hell. How my faith in God survived I do not know, unless it was that Father Cassidy had laid the foundation of a belief in the God of Love that was stronger and deeper than this new doctrine of a God of Retribution as presented in the annual three days' retreat.

I have heard it said that many Stonyhurst boys leave the Church when they go out into the world. In our family Charles did, and so did my brother Frank, but they both returned in later life. Whether it is true of others I don't know, but I am convinced that the intensive propaganda of the annual three days' spiritual retreat was liable to do more harm than good.

There was really no need for such intensive propaganda, the daily influence of our Jesuit teachers was sufficient. In my time there were over sixty Jesuit priests and postulants, all dedicated men and some of them highly intelligent. It was the dedication that conveyed the message. All our written work had to have at the top of the page the heading A.M.D.G. – "Ad Majoram Dei Gloriam", (translated, "To the greater glory of God"). Its meaning was above my head, but the time comes in later life when one realises the profound principle that is expressed. It is sad that under modern conditions so few people feel in a position to accept it in their daily work.

Life in other directions at Stonyhurst was probably much as in other public schools. To enjoy life one had to run with the pack, be good at games and follow the popular line. In these directions I was a miserable failure – no good at games and inclined to run against the tide. So I had to take the consequences in the form of too many scraps. They were not of sufficient intensity to be called full-blooded fights. At home Driscoll, one of the lounge waiters, was a boxer. He offered to teach me and I became his pupil. It was useful; I learnt to defend myself and also how to take the offensive. Back at college it was worth-while, as I was able to give a better account of myself. I followed it up in the college gymnasium and entered the boxing competitions. In one of them I got a hammering, after which I adjourned to the indoor swimming bath where I squatted in the shallow end aching all over and bleeding. My blood turned the shallow end a faint pink – it was quite impressive.

Most of the time I was living in a world of books. It had started at Hodder where I discovered Henty and Marryat. After that I graduated from one author to another, Stanley Weyman, Anthony Hope, Rider Haggard, Conan Doyle, Stevenson, W. W. Jacobs, Walter Scott, Charles Dickens, Jeffrey Farnol, George A. Birmingham, and those two marvellous books, *Lorna Doone* and *Robbery Under Arms*, the latter still being one of my favourites. My reading blotted out all the drabness. I was transported and entered completely into the worlds their authors had created, so much so that I was able to ignore the obnoxious sides of college life.

With four years difference in our ages, Charles and I did not see much of each other. Towards the end of his time at Stonyhurst, Charles was chosen to play a small part in *The Private Secretary* by Charles Hawtrey. The plays were staged in the college Academy Room. Sitting at the back of the large hall and looking down towards the stage, I felt intensely involved and in a state of acute anxiety; but once he appeared the agony was over — he was so astonishingly good. It was my first experience of the first nights of Charles, and I never got over my feeling of anxiety. Charles was usually in an agony of nervousness, and it always communicated itself to me.

We were only a year together at the college — he left in 1915 and I left in 1919. Charles left to go to London to gain experience in the hotel business, working at Claridge's Hotel for two years and leaving there to join the forces in 1917. On the rare occasions when he came home from Claridge's he talked of nothing but the theatre, describing the shows he had seen, nearly always from the gallery. He saw revues with Nelson Keys, Nat. D. Ayer and Alice Delysia. *Chu Chin Chow* was his favourite show; he saw it thirteen times. Gerald du Maurier became one of his heroes. His interest infected me, and he took me to see a travelling company performing *The Bing Boys*. I found it

amusing but it had rather strange consequences. Back at
Stonyhurst I wrote a parody of *The Bing Boys*, innocently
using a pretty young boy in place of the heroine, and one
of the senior boys (who in college acted as a protector to
his young protégé) as the hero. In my parody they sang
together the song "If you were the only girl in the world",
but in this case it was "If you were the only boy in the
world and I was the only man". Had I been better informed
and more sophisticated I would have realised that I was
writing up a homosexual situation. The one and only copy
of the parody, written in an exercise book, passed from
hand to hand. It was quite a success, so successful that it
arrived into the hands of one of the Jesuits, who gave me
credit for a more scurrilous wit than I deserved. Eventually
my class master, a Father Bartlett, was called into consultation. He was a red-faced hearty man, known by the boys as
"The Beetroot". He suspected the extent of my ignorance.
We had a curious interview with my dog-eared manuscript
on the table — it must have convinced him of my inno-
cence. He finished by warning me to be careful of writing
about real people; it was generous on his part, as in the
script there was a rumbustious character who could easily
have been mistaken for him. My manuscript was confisca-
ted, and after that I heard no more about it.

About this time I discovered that a private study of my
own was a possibility. It was something worth working for,
anything to get out of the communal dormitories, and to
have a place where I would be able to read to my heart's
content. The first step to a private study was to be put into
a small dormitory holding ten boys, which was occupied
by those in line for a room of their own. One of the boys
in the dormitory was an expert in sound effects. He would
fill his chamber pot with water, and after lights out he
would produce the most remarkable expressive noises by
groaning and wheezing, dropping one or two pieces of soap
with a "plop, plop" into his chamber pot, finishing with

an ecstatic sigh of relief. He would have made a magnificent sound radio producer, but he joined the Church, and the last time I heard of him he was a bishop.

Soon after I got my private study I was chosen to be one of the readers to the community of Jesuits whilst they were eating their lunch. They lunched in silence; the reader entered the dining room, bowed to the rector, and took the chosen book to the readers' desk. It was always an interesting book and once I had got over my nervousness I found it enjoyable, so much so that I vaguely wondered whether I might have a vocation for the monastic life. It was a period when I was anxiously looking to the future, finding it difficult to conceive how I should be able to make a living. I was looking to the religious life as a haven from the uncertainty of the outside world.

Life was much more attractive with the privacy of a study of my own. I was working hard, reading every moment of my spare time and far into the night — it can't have done me any good. I ruined my eyesight, and I began to look in very poor shape. Mother was so concerned that she called the doctor in to examine me. He was not satisfied, so a consultant physician was called in. The final diagnosis was that I had tubercular glands in my stomach and was in generally poor condition. The prescribed course of action was that I should leave school, have a period of rest and recuperation, and after that the doctors advised that I should live an open-air life.

The result was that I had to leave Stonyhurst without having passed any exams, and with no hope of going to a university. By this time I had reached a stage when I was vaguely hoping to go to university to study law, and after that to read for the bar; now all thoughts of this had to be abandoned. My leaving was involuntary, as when I left for the holidays I had no idea that I was not to return. It was a stage at which school life was becoming more bearable, but only after several years of comparative misery. I have vivid memories of being wretchedly cold and existing on food that was only just eatable. I was emerging into better conditions when, in the year 1919 at sixteen years of age, I had to leave.

CHAPTER III

ON THE YORKSHIRE WOLDS

The hotel was no place in which to recuperate, so I was
sent to live with my Aunt Mary – Mrs. Mary Harrison. She
was a widow, my father's sister and she lived at Burniston,
a village three miles north of Scarborough where she had a
cottage with a garden. Aunt Mary was a Bohemian character with a passion for collecting and, like my father, she was
a very good gardener. She was tall and buxom, with a face
that radiated pleasure and good will; Charles and I adored
her. She had little money but an excellent eye which she
used to great effect. She frequented the sale rooms and
would sometimes return in triumph with some treasure,
which she had probably acquired for a very small price.
The result was that her cottage was full of beautiful things.
We lived an irregular life, meals being moveable feasts,
always tasty and good, prepared and cooked when the
spirit moved her and liable to be served on a table
covered by newspaper.

Mother did not approve of Aunt Mary, who was too
Bohemian for her tastes and might be a bad influence
on her boys. She was right about the influence but
wrong in thinking it bad. Aunt Mary infected both Charles
and myself with her passion for collecting. She would
acquire anything she could afford that she thought
beautiful. As I write in my study, I can look at a
pair of rare Staffordshire Kylins which Aunt Mary
bought sixty-five years ago. When she bought them
they were covered with thick dark paint. She had realised
that underneath the paint there were the rich colours of
the Staffordshire glaze, so she spent hours patiently chipping

the paint away with a pin until the original colours of the glaze were uncovered. There was a Baptist Chapel across the road from her cottage, and alongside the Chapel lived John Jackson. He was the moving spirit in the congregation – a sprightly little man full of life and a remarkable preacher. People came from miles around to hear him. He was a friend of Aunt Mary, and when he heard that I was to be in the village for some time he invited me to attend his services. It was as good as going to the theatre, as the lay preachers sometimes spoke in the vernacular, one I remember was describing the joys of heaven. "Why", he said, "when yer gets to 'eaven, there'll be mountains of pudden and rivers of broth". The same man describing the story of Zaccheus climbing up the thorn tree to see the passing of Jesus, and of his falling out of the tree as He passed, used another vivid metaphor – "He fell out o't tree and rived 'is britches' ass out". The lay preachers were much better than the circuit ministers, who spoke well but did not use such vivid language.

I spent a wonderful spring and summer at Burniston. At the foot of my Aunt's garden there was a small trout stream, the banks of which teemed with wild life. Father would come to see us, and we would wander up the stream together. He knew the owner of the farm, who gave him permission to fish, and there he used to teach me the rudiments of fly fishing. By the river were nests of wild duck, water hens, dippers, long-tailed tits and many other birds to give interest to our quiet expeditions. Walking along the stream father broached the question of my future. The doctors had suggested that for reasons of health I ought to go in for an open-air life, so he asked me whether I would like to be a farmer. The summer with Aunt Mary mostly spent in the open air, had been a wonderfully happy experience. I knew nothing of farming and I had never thought of it as a way of life; but now the idea of a life spent in country surroundings made a great appeal.

Father's idea was that I should spend the winter at his farm in Lockton on the edge of the Yorkshire Moors. The farm was let to a tenant, Mr. Palfreyman. Father stayed there for two nights a week throughout the shooting season. He suggested that in the following year I should leave Lockton to become a farm pupil at some larger farm, to train seriously. Whatever father suggested I was ready to agree to, so it was arranged that in September I should move to Lockton.

"Cherry Tree Farm" was at the entrance to Lockton village, a characteristic moorland type of stone building, with oak beams and wide thick oak planking. Father arranged that I should have his bedroom, which was wood panelled with a fine old hob grate. I was to be looked after by Mrs. Palfreyman and fed as one of the family. There was plenty of home-cured bacon and ham, lashings of eggs, a joint of beef or mutton each week – every day home-baked bread, scones and cakes; butter, milk and cream from the farm dairy. During the shooting season we had pheasant, partridge, grouse, rabbits and hares – everything prepared and cooked by Mrs. Palfreyman. Before the winter was over, all idea of my being delicate seemed to have vanished.

Most of my time was spent with Harland, father's part-time gamekeeper. He was a tall gaunt man with unusual poise and dignity. He had a cogent way of expressing himself with a use of English that was all his own. He loved my father and I benefited from their relationship. Harland had started life as a coachman. He was used to dealing with the gentry, and he did his best to convert me to the mould. Father commissioned him to teach me to shoot. We would go out together, he carrying his twelve-bore shotgun and I carrying a lighter twenty-bore which father had bought me. For the purpose of shooting lessons, anything moving was fair game to Harland.

One of his jobs was to look after a crocodile that lived in

the glass hot-house of a property in an adjoining village. When he wanted me to have a go at some inoffensive water hen he would rap out, "Shoot it for the croc", and if I managed to hit it, in it would go into his shooting bag to be fed to the crocodile later. He once even suggested that I should shoot at a bat. "Shoot it, Mr. Tom", he exclaimed — I protested, "Shoot a bat — what's wrong with a bat?" Harland paused for thought and eventually came out with, "A bat, a bat is the worst thing you can have in a church tower", and stalked on in moody silence.

One day we had been out rabbit shooting together. On our return we passed mother sitting in the garden reading her Missal. Harland believed in being polite to ladies, so he held up a rabbit for mother to see and said to her, "That's a fine buck rabbit, Mum". Without thinking mother replied, "How can you tell it's a buck rabbit, Harland?" There was a pause, "By examination, Mum", was Harland's considered reply.

That winter I was allowed to go out shooting with father and Harland. The shoot was a rough shoot that produced partridge, pheasant, hares and rabbits and an occasional grouse and woodcock. It was fairly extensive, I estimate that it was well over a thousand acres, mostly consisting of small farms, with small fields and wooded valleys on the east and west boundaries. Father always had good gun dogs, spaniels and retrievers. Both Harland and he were good shots, so that often the bag was substantial and made a valuable addition to the hotel larder. Although not much of it was contributed by me, I enjoyed the day's shooting, but I was never a good shot.

I spent a winter and the following summer at Lockton. By then father had found a farmer, Tom Mitchell of Enthorpe Farm near Goodmanham on the Yorkshire Wolds, who was willing to take me on as a farm pupil. It was arranged that I should go to Enthorpe at the beginning of October. Enthorpe was a fair sized farm of something over five hundred acres, on the estate of the Earl of Londes-borough. Tom Mitchell was a bachelor living with his mother. Old Mrs. Mitchell was a formidable lady, whose principal interest seemed to be the Court news as reported in the *Yorkshire Post*. There was another farm pupil older than myself called Spragg, who was working in the sheep-fold. I was put under Spragg's wing. In those days the Yorkshire Wolds was great sheep country. In the winter the young sheep were folded on white turnips, and later swedes, on which they were fattened with a supplementary diet of corn and sheep cake made from crushed linseed. A piece of turnip field was enclosed by two lines of wire netting supported by five foot wooden stakes. The lines of nets ran parallel, one hundred to two hundred yards apart. Between the two lines of wire netting a fresh fold was set every day by band nets each fifty yards long and set on similar stakes. The stakes were driven into the ground by the use of a shaped iron bar, known as a gavlock, and the fifty yards long band nets were set along the rows of stakes. Each day a fresh fold was set, a line of nets was un-hitched from the stakes, then picked off the ground on to a stake by carrying the stake in both hands with the two ends protruding, so that the net could be happed up onto it like a huge piece of knitting.

Every day half the turnips in the next day's fold had to be torn out of the ground by a turnip pick, the roots cleaned off by a turnip knife and the turnip knocked off the pick by striking the pick on the back of the knife, so that the cleaned turnips were tossed into a succession of heaps, along the side of which the next day's line of band nets were to be set. Then when the sheep were let into the fresh fold, the heaped turnips were sliced by a hand-turned turnip cutter and fed into troughs twice a day. It was a hard grinding routine for the shepherds, bearable in fine weather, but dreadful in wet weather. It was a wet spell when I started and the unaccustomed physical effort almost got the better of me. My clothing wouldn't keep out the weather — the wet seemed to work in even through the heaviest waterproofs. I ached in every limb and every muscle, my teeth came loose and it seemed just a question of time before I would have to give in. There were some jobs that were beyond my strength. I couldn't gather up the wet fifty yard long band nets on to a stake, they were too heavy for me and I couldn't manage the iron gavlock — but I struggled on. The wet weather seemed as though it would never end; when the sun did come it was like paradise. Gradually I became acclimatised and before the end of the winter there was not a job in the sheepfold that I could not turn my hand to.

As the winter wore on, drafts of the fat young sheep were sent to the market or sold to visiting sheep dealers, until by the spring there were only the ewes in lamb left. Spragg moved on to other work, and I was left to help the shepherd during lambing time. The ewes were taken from the sheep-fold and put onto the permanent pasture land. A lambing yard with separate lambing pens was built with thick walls of straw held up by wire netting, and inside the yard separate pens made with wood hurdles. Every day the experienced eye of the shepherd picked out the ewes due to lamb and herded them into the lambing yard where they were kept until they had lambed. Once the lambs were on their feet, the ewes with one, two or three spindly lambs, were put out to a special pasture kept ready to receive them. There was a shepherd's hut standing near the lambing yard, in which the shepherd spent the night, every now and then going out with his lantern to see that all was well. The ewes were never left by the shepherd, he was gentleness itself. Sometimes a birth would start with the lamb coming the wrong way. He was able to re-arrange the position of the lamb in the womb, so that once the lamb was coming head and forefeet first the birth was successfully accomplished.

Occasionally a ewe would have triplets and only sufficient milk for two; then the extra lamb would be palmed off onto the next ewe that had only one lamb. The shepherd would cover the unwanted lamb with the after-birth of the ewe with only one, so that when the ewe got to her feet to lick her newly born she found two instead of one. It was an anxious moment, for the ewes were difficult to deceive, but once they had taken to a lamb they would always look after it.

If I had any doubts about adopting a farming life, they vanished in that lambing yard. To be accepted by the sheep as one of their natural guardians was a deeply satisfying experience.

Spring and summer on the farm were lovely seasons. It was before the day of tractors; the land was worked by horses. There were eight pairs of horses at Enthorpe, each pair in charge of a horseman. The leading horseman known as the waggoner was the right hand man of the farm fore-man. In the autumn and in the spring, teams of horses would go in procession from the stable to the field that was being worked; the near horse of each pair carried the horseman sitting with his legs dangling down the near side, the pro-cession sedately plodding on with harness jangling. Each pair of horses was the responsibility of the horseman that worked them and each horseman took a pride in the condition of his pair.

When the lambing was over, the shepherd could manage on his own, so that I came to do other simple jobs. Harrowing the seed corn in, sometimes taking a cart with supplies to the field — all easy jobs. There are so many jobs on a farm that can only be done by highly skilled men. Ploughing, hedging, scruffling, milking, shearing, corn-stack building and many other things. Gradually I wormed my way into some of them. At shearing time my job was to catch the ewes and hand them to the shearers, until at length one said, "Come on, lad, have a go". I managed, but it was a long time before I could turn a ewe down with a clean creamy uncut skin and without untidy lumps of wool left all over it.

One of the warmest summer jobs was hoeing and singling the turnips. Miles and miles of rows of young turnip plants had to be gapped with a hoe, leaving a single plant to each eighteen inches. We worked in a gang, at the rate of progress set by the foreman. It was a killing job for me attempting to keep pace. The sun beating down on the back of our necks, heads bent, eyes down, "chop, chop, chop", backs aching. I was working as though my life depended upon it, determined to hold my own and not to be a drag on the team.

At this time of the year the cart horses were put out to grass. Each evening after their work, they were stripped of their harness in the stable and sent off with a slap on their great shining rumps. They galloped like children released from school, rearing, kicking, neighing, farting – a great sight and a great sound, into their pasture where they settled down to enjoy the summer evening.

One of my jobs was stacking the straw on threshing days. The straw spewed out of the thresher on to the hopper of the elevator, up the elevator and poured down on to me, whilst I was frantically trying to build a tall stack that would stand firm without wobbling over. It was a lonely job, and for some reason a great thought provoker. On my own on top of the mounting stack, my thoughts would turn towards the future. How was I going to make a success of my farming life? In those days the farmers were doing badly, so if the experienced men I knew could scarcely make a living, how was I going to manage? That's where I went wrong, instead of thinking of how I was going to make a good farmer, I was worrying about how I was going to make money. Idea after idea came into my mind, including the one I eventually adopted which was to combine farming with agricultural auctioneering. From the point of view of making money it was a good idea, from the point of view of living a satisfactory life, a bad one.

Harvest time brought my farming year full cycle. I had arrived at Enthorpe in October, the corn stubbles were being ploughed to be worked in the spring. I had seen the young corn shading the brown fields with green, until they became a sea of green flowing in the wind, gradually turning to rich gold. The Yorkshire Wolds are mostly light land on chalk, gently sloping from one horizon to the next – vast fields, small hedges, dew ponds here and there, that by some miracle gather and hold water without any streams to feed them. What a country to be in at harvest time! The corn was cut by horse drawn cutters and binders that threw out the corn bound into sheaves. The sheaves were lifted and stooked; each stook held about twelve sheaves clapped together so that they stood upright to dry in the wind. Then when the sheaves were ready, the corn was lifted. Forked on to the boat-shaped pole waggons, each waggoner skilfully building a great load of the sheaves that wound its way back to the stackyard like a ship sailing on dry land.

In the stackyard the sheaves were forked from the waggons on to the rising stack, a man building the stack sheaf by sheaf rising as a massive shape, symmetrical, balanced – a work of extraordinary skill. I know no finer sight than a well filled stackyard, full of thatched corn stacks, incredibly solid and satisfying. It was hard work in harvest time but there was a carefree spirit. The horsemen would race the waggons back from the stackyard to the field, trotting down the narrow cart tracks, and even breaking into a gallop across the stubbles, harness jangling, waggons heaving and groaning behind the sweating horses. We were all imbued with a sense of urgency, and when at last it was over with a sense of communal achievement.

The following winter I was back in the sheep-fold. This time I was able to handle the iron gavlock, set the nets, clean the turnips and handle the turnip cutter. I had become the right hand man to the shepherd. Not only the shepherd accepted me, but also the sheep – the sheep that I had helped to lamb. When I was in the sheep-fold some of them would follow me about, sometimes gently butting me with their heads. Most people think that sheep are all to a pattern, but this is not true. There is just as much difference in their faces as there is in the faces of humans and a great deal of difference in their characters. Some are bold and playful, even affectionate, others are shy and withdrawn, and some are aggressive.

By this time the shepherd was treating me as a friend and confidant. He was a Rabelaisian character, single, but very interested in women. In the summer he had a woman friend from a nearby town who used to visit him in his moveable shepherd's hut. The hut was on four wheels standing about eighteen inches clear of the ground, having two loose floorboards. He would escort her to the hut, lock her in from the outside, and then enter the hut from the bottom through the two loose floorboards. It must have been an exciting encounter.

There were occasional village "hops" during one of which I noticed him solemnly proceeding round the room with a girl in his arms and with a set expression on his face. The following day when we were working together I mentioned this to him and enquired what he had been thinking about. "Why, lad," he replied, "Ah'm wondering if their knickers have buttons down t'side or elastic round t'top".

I stayed with him right through the winter and through the lambing time. He taught me one or two things beside shepherding. How to snickle a rabbit, how to spot the regular tracks of a hare, and how to set a snickle high to catch it between bounds. In summer the farm lads would look out for the nests of wood pigeons and if they could be reached they would climb up the tree and tie a band around the nestlings' leg, so that when they were fat and ready to fly away they could be collected off the nest for the pot. The farm was teeming with game. The shepherd had a very cunning way of getting a pheasant. He would entice them into an enclosed yard by regularly putting down corn and then he would insert barley horns through the grains of corn so that the corn would stick in the throat of the pheasant.

The farm lads knew where the pheasants roosted, they would put down corn in the vicinity and when they saw that it was being taken they would put down corn soaked in whisky. The pheasants would take it, then too drunk to fly up into the trees to their roosting perches, stagger around until the farm lads picked them up and wrung their necks. Their pay was so poor that they had to supplement their diet as best they could. On thick misty days I would take the gun out and do my part to swell their secret larder.

I had learnt to ride horseback and I rode every Sunday to Houghton Hall the other side of Market Weighton, where there was a Roman Catholic church. Spragg, the other pupil, was a good horseman, and my teacher. Close beside Enthorpe there was a tiny station on a little branch railway line and sometimes farmers would ride over to take the train there, leaving their horses in our stables. It was generally on a market day, when Tom Mitchell our boss was also away. We used to try them all out, have a gallop round the farm and give them a good rub down to remove the evidence before the farmers' return. It was good practice for me but not without mishap, as one day I was thrown off into the stable yard pond.

The following spring one of the horse lads fell ill, it was seed time when every pair of horses counted. Tom Mitchell suggested that I should take on the missing horseman's pair of horses until he returned from hospital. It was no easy job, I could scarcely reach up to get the great stuffed leather collars over the horses' heads. The horses knew I was a

novice and they played me up. I didn't speak the right
language, my "Git up", "Gee Warve", "Gee back" and
"Whoa there" were not delivered in the rich East Riding
brogue, which was the only tongue they understood. One
day, ploughing light land on a hillside, the plough sock
bumping along the white chalk, I was going well with the
furrow horse steadily plodding so that the furrow was
turning over straight as a die; I couldn't help bursting into
triumphant song.

The horsemen were all young single men living in the
Hinds' House at the back of the main farmhouse, boarded
by the foreman and his wife. They were not able to marry
until they got a job that carried a house with it. Their
conversation was mostly on women and horses, and round
about the farm buildings scribbled in odd places, there were
crude sayings, rhymes and rough drawings that spoke elo-
quently of their frustration. The conversation the morning
after a village hop was on the happenings of the previous
evening. They had the village girls weighed up, and very
little was left to the imagination.

I took it all in avidly, my sex education having begun
in the lambing yard, continued with the shepherd, and
with the horsemen spelling it out in crude but expressive
language. With the animal sex life of the farm bursting out
all over, I began to understand what it was about, and
longed for the time when I should get some practical
experience for myself.

CHAPTER IV

FARMING AND AUCTIONEERING

My time at Enthorpe was drawing to an end. Father had gone along with my idea of combining agricultural auctioneering with farming and he had found an auctioneer and farmer, Mr. John Murray of Hulam Farm, Castle Eden, County Durham, who was willing to take me as a pupil. His family firm had auction marts at Castle Eden, Stockton and Seaham Harbour, farms at Castle Eden and Seaham Harbour, also hill farms on the Northumberland hills north of Haltwhistle. The arrangement was that I was to live at Hulam Farm with John Murray and his wife, and I was to work as a pupil and personal assistant to John, who was the senior partner in the family firm.

It was sad leaving Enthorpe, where I seemed to have become an entirely different person with completely changed interests. It had all happened without any mental effort, just in the natural course of living an open-air farm life. More important, I had arrived at Enthorpe a weakling, now I was leaving fit and healthy. I didn't know at the time how much I had to be thankful for, the life at Enthorpe was the foundation of the good health that I have enjoyed ever since. It had re-inforced the love of country life and country pursuits which I had first got from my father, and after the three years at Enthorpe I have never lost it.

Hulam was a great change. It was a large mixed farm on the edge of a pit district. There were herds of pedigree cattle, pedigree pigs, and two flocks of pedigree sheep — Border Leicesters and the black-faced Oxfords. The farm was secondary to the agricultural auctioneering and valueing. Four or five days a week John Murray would be either at the auction mart, conducting farm sales or doing farm valuations. He took me with him as a clerk and personal assistant.

It was a new world dominated by money. The princes of the auction mart were cattle dealers, large butchers and co-operative buyers, who seemed to be engaged in a constant battle of wits. On the rostrum the auctioneer dominated the scene, trying to hold the balance between the sellers and the buyers, whilst the cattle, sheep and pigs were mere pawns, unregarded and sometimes ill-treated in the all-important game of making money. It was a horrible, brutal world, which I am afraid I must have taken to, as after a few months the firm took out an auctioneer's licence on my behalf so that I could sell in the sheep ring of the Stockton auction mart.

The farm valuations were the most interesting part of the work. In that district much of the land had coal pits underneath. The coal seams had a damaging effect on the crops above, so that the farmers claimed compensation from the owners of the coal pits. At certain seasons of the year we were travelling all over the country assessing and agreeing damages with a valuer acting on behalf of the mine owners. One valuation that I remember was in open country, on which we were told a large chemical factory was to be built. It was the site for the huge I.C.I. plant at Billingham.

Back at the farm my principal interest was the sheep. The shepherd, Jim Ferguson, was a Scotsman from the border country, a gentle upright and altogether first class man and, like all good countrymen, dignified and self-assured, the complete antithesis to the sharp characters I was meeting at the markets. When he found that I was interested in sheep Jim took me under his wing. He had a black and white border collie called "Jed", a most skilful and clever bitch with an uncanny gift of anticipation when it came to shepherding. She seemed to know exactly where and when the sheep would make a dash for it. In her spare time she would amuse herself by gently shepherding hens from one end of the farmyard to the other, just by lying in strategic places, and seeming to will them to go to the place that she had chosen for them. My happiest times at Hulam were spent with Jim and his dog.

Jim's special interest was the flock of Border Leicesters. They are a most aristocratic breed of sheep, with Roman-nosed heads set on curved necks, fine boned limbs and with beautiful fleeces. The Hulam flock was one of the best in the area. Jim enlisted my help to prepare them for the show-ring and for the ram sales. I became skilful at shaping the fleeces. They were prepared by special dips and delicate clipping, just as carefully as a woman prepares her coiffure for some important occasion. Jim and I became firm friends. We travelled together with the sheep to the shows and in the show-rings I was allowed to parade the second string. Back at the farm, Jim taught me how to feed sheep for the fat stock shows; his secret being to keep them on good pasture and give them feeds of crushed oats and sheep cake, a little at a time, but as often as possible.

John Murray took me up to the hill farm lying low in a fold of the Northumberland hills. It was miles from any-where, surrounded by green moorland with boggy little trout streams. The farm was stocked with a flock of black-faced moorland sheep, and a herd of black Galloway cows running with a white Shorthorn bull. The fires were made with peat cut and dried on the farm. Our visit was in the spring, as in winter the farm was liable to be cut off by snow for weeks at a time. When we were there the Galloway cows had calved and were grazing out on the green moor-land, with their calves running with them. The young black-faced rams spent much of their time fighting; they were on pasture close to the farm. Facing one another and each stepping back for as much as twenty yards they would suddenly charge head down. When their skulls met the crack could be heard for miles. Occasionally the stronger of the two would break the neck of the weaker one so that it dropped down stone dead. No wonder the black-faced sheep are such a hardy race.

John was a judge of anything on four legs. I have been with him at a country show where he not only judged the sheep but also the pigs and the cattle. He would have been just as capable of judging the horses. All his own stock were of good quality. He taught me that the approach of a judge of animals of any kind is very similar to the approach of a connoisseur of art.

That was the saving aspect of my life at Castle Eden — living with the judgement of such an experienced man. Auctioneering was a different matter; there everything was a case of immediate and temporary values, with farmers anxiously bringing in their stock hoping to meet a good market, and dealers, fast talkers looking for bargains, anything for a quick profit. It was a world where the buyer must beware. Milking cows were got up specially for sale, washed and groomed with their udders bursting with milk, the teats having been unnaturally sealed to give them the appearance of being prolific milkers, irrespective of the pain and discomfort to the animal. The sellers and buyers were in and out of the public houses sealing bargains with a drink. Brutal drovers were driving the cattle from pen to sales ring and at the end of the market from the pens to the slaughter-house. I didn't see it that way at the time, all my energies were taken up in absorbing the strange new world, learning to weigh up the market value of animals at a glance, and thinking of them solely in terms of money. It was only in my leisure time, which was mostly spent with the shepherd Jim Ferguson, that I retained a sense of lasting quality and value. The two years I spent at Hulam widened my knowledge of the commercial farming world, but lessened my grip on straightforward farming. I was selling every week in the Stockton sheep ring and beginning to enjoy the manipulation of the trade. I was able to judge the value of each pen of sheep as it came into the ring, confidently starting off the bidding and trotting it sometimes against a single bidder until it was approaching somewhere near its market value. There were times when I found myself left without a genuine bid; on those occasions the lot would be knocked down to one of the dealers, who in return would be given a quick knock later, to compensate him for helping me out of my difficulty. At farm sales, John Murray would sometimes use me as a relief auctioneer to deal with some of the less important items. During the valuation season he would encourage me to make my own independent valuations, so that I could compare them with the figures of the more experienced men.

Father had bought me a motorcycle so that I could get back home. The hotel was going well but there were difficulties. When Charles was demobilised at the end of the war, he returned to help to run the family business. He was not settling and he was not caring for the life. My parents were disappointed, especially mother. For her the Pavilion was everything; the customers sacred beings who had to be satisfied at all costs. Not so for Charles. Customers to him were a source of interest, creatures to be studied rather than beings to be pleased. He had devastating powers of mimicry, finding in the staff an appreciative audience, who recognised in his cameo performances brilliant cartoons of some of their tormentors.

It was obvious that Charles was not made for the business, and that there was an unhappy situation developing between mother, father and him. Not so much father, because he was ill and he was losing touch. Mother complained that Charles was more interested in amateur theatricals than in the hotel business — which indeed he was. He couldn't bring himself to get up early and do the shopping; he wasn't interested in the catering, the customers interested and amused him, but he wasn't prepared to dance attendance on them.

He looked on the hotel more as a production than a daily service, but he was gradually transforming the décor and the character of the place. When he came back from the war, it was a comfortable old fashioned Victorian hotel. Charles made it both attractive and lively, but he was letting the quality of the service and the catering slip.

When I came home for brief visits, both mother and Charles would pour out their troubles – mother finding Charles difficult to deal with, Charles longing to be rid of his unwanted responsibilities. By this time farming had not the same attraction for me. If I had stayed on at Enthorpe, and from there moved to a farm of my own, it would have been different. At Enthorpe I was developing a vocational attitude to the farming life, whereas at Hulam I was keen enough, but it was only a keenness to make money. Anyway, one day when Charles tackled me I was ready to listen.

He had reached a point when he could stand the hotel life no longer. His one interest was the stage. It had been his dominating influence from childhood. As a little boy he had had his own toy theatre, at Stonyhurst his greatest success had been in the school play, and in London, when he was training for the hotel business at Claridges, all his spare money and every moment he could afford was spent on the cheap seats of the London theatres. He still spoke of Gerald du Maurier as his hero, Hilda Trevelyan and Alice Delysia as his heroines. After the war, back at home, he had only really come to life working for the amateur stage. Just before he tackled me, he had had an outstanding success playing Willie Mossop in *Hobson's Choice* with a local amateur production. He was determined to leave home and try his luck on the stage. "Would I agree to come back home and take his place in the business?" If I would, father and mother had promised that if he was accepted, he could go to the Royal Academy of Dramatic Art in Gower Street, London.

I was shocked. It seemed such a drastic step for Charles, to forego what amounted to his inheritance as the eldest son for such a precarious life, and for me to take his place in the family business. As I thought it could only be a temporary obsession, I told him I would take his place until he came back home. "I shall never come back home to the business, Tom; I would starve in the gutter first" was his reply.

So it was arranged. Charles was accepted by the Royal Academy of Dramatic Art, and within three years he was playing leads in the West End. I returned home and took to the hotel business as though it had been my natural vocation.

CHAPTER V

IN AT THE DEEP END

Shortly before I returned home, in 1924, my father's health had grown rapidly worse. He died suddenly, soon after it had been decided that Charles should try his luck on the stage.

Father was not an ambitious man. He would have been content to remain at the Victoria, where he had set up house with mother when they were married. It was the determination of mother to rise in the world and to be able to give her children a good education, that had dictated the move to the Pavilion. For father the result had been years of financial worry, the disruption of his family life and it had imposed on him a way of living for which he did not care. The move proved financially successful and we children received the benefit; but the worry and the struggle shortened father's life. He was only fifty-five years of age when he died.

With father dead, mother prostrate with shock, Charles training for the stage in London, at the age of twenty-one I was left in charge of the hotel with no one to guide me. Fortunately, the staff knew their job and they knew me, as I had grown up with many of them. One change was that instead of calling me "Young Tommy", I was given the title of "Mr. Tom". From the staff point of view, the main difference was that for a time they had lost the keen surveillance of my mother and they were now dealing with Mr. Tom in place of Mr. Charles.

I was soon engrossed in the atmosphere of the hotel, as though I had never been away from it. In one way it was fortunate that I had no one to guide me and that I had to find my feet and gain self-confidence. The only thing I knew anything about was the marketing, as my shopping expeditions with father had made a lasting impression. My farming and auctioneering experiences had deepened my interest in quality. The kitchens were in charge of Chef Moore, an Englishman who over the years was to prove himself one of the finest chefs in the country. He was delighted when I re-started my father's shopping routine and we soon re-established the tradition that only the best would be accepted in the Pavilion kitchens.

I gradually learnt from Chef Moore the essentials of kitchen management, he taught me the part that I must play in the catering organisation, particularly the need for my supervision of the service of meals. We were catering for a critical audience — Yorkshire people are very demanding when it comes to food. I soon found out how demanding they could be, when one evening roast pheasant had been served as the main course of the dinner. After the dinner was over, one of the customers, a manufacturer from Leeds, sent for me to go to his bedroom. He had been served with a tough portion of pheasant; he went for me until he reduced me to tears, starting with the ominous words: "It won't do, mi lad, it won't do", and before he finished he had predicted disaster and bankruptcy. It was a pity that he was not dealing with Charles; he would have stored it up and one day it would have come out on the stage or on the screen in one of his performances.

The hotel I took over from Charles was very different from the hotel he had taken over from my parents. At the end of the 1914-1918 war the Pavilion was a comfortable old-fashioned hotel, but before he left for London in 1924, Charles was transforming it into an hotel that entertained the guests as well as feeding and making them comfortable. He had started to change the atmosphere of the interior. He had found a young London decorator, John

Hill, an intelligent man of taste and a good designer, who could adapt his work to the special needs of the hotel business. His work was giving the hotel a distinguished character. I continued to work with John and we worked together throughout my hotel career up to the time of my retirement.

The principal innovation in the time of Charles was his importation of a lounge and dance band for the holiday season, led by a young pianist called Harry Tait. Harry was a talented musician, extremely good looking, with a pleasant but somewhat aloof personality. His music transformed the hotel; it gave it a festive atmosphere which permeated both the guests and the staff. Charles blossomed in the atmosphere he had created. He was not satisfied with the usual staid hotel dances, so he organized for peak holiday periods fetes, for which the ballroom was decorated to a theme, the band dressed in special costumes, and elaborate paper favours, imported from Paris, were distributed to the guests. The distribution of the favours created a furore; they were frantically sought after, as though they were articles of priceless value.

Charles had realised that hotels should sell pleasure rather than be merely utilitarian institutions and I inherited this belief, much to my advantage. It was sound policy. Charles had placed the decorations in the hands of John Hill, but I had a part to play in it. As each room was decorated there was a need for a painting or some objet d'art as a focal point; up to my arrival these had been collected by Charles; now it was my responsibility. I knew nothing of such things, but here again the influence of Charles helped me.

He had left behind his friend Bruce Turner. Bruce was a little-known artist, whom Charles had met through some amateur theatrical production and he had made a friend of him. He used to invite him to stay at the hotel as his guest. I had met him several times during the period I was farming, so when I came back to the hotel I continued to entertain him as Charles had done. Bruce was a wraith of a man, tall and bent, pale and bespectacled, a Zen Buddhist; he was always peering into a world of which most of us are completely unconscious. He had been a conscientious objector during the war and had been called up and forced into uniform, so brutally that in the process his arm had been broken. He was imprisoned in Armley gaol, where his health had been ruined, but not his spirit. His two main interests were philosophy and art. The expression of his thoughts was too abstruse for me, far above my young head, but I conceived an admiration for him, and we established a master-pupil relationship. It was Bruce who laid the foundations of my interest in art, convincing me that the most important human beings are the creative artists — a belief that I hold to this day. It was through Bruce that I started to collect paintings. He spoke at length on Cézanne, Van Gogh, Gauguin, Courbet and Manet and he encouraged me to go to the galleries to see their work.

In the meantime my collecting was concerned with buying small paintings for the bedrooms, such things as Landseer sketches, eighteenth and nineteenth century pastels, Gaudier-Brzeska drawings, most of which were selected for their decorative quality rather than their artistic merit. They were not always appreciated. In my early days in the hotel, I was passing along a bedroom corridor when I was accosted by a customer, who drew me back into his bedroom. He pointed to a small portrait sketch by Duncan Grant of a woman with a swan-like neck. "Did you ever see a woman with a neck like that?", he asked. "Never mind", I replied gently, "I will give you another bedroom".

One painting that I hung temporarily had an unexpected effect. I had commissioned Bruce Turner to design the decorations for a men's smokeroom bar. The scheme included one of his paintings as the focal point. The painting was not ready in time, so I temporarily hung one of my own paintings — a portrait by Matthew Smith of Vera Cunningham. I had purchased it for myself from Tooth, the Bond Street art dealer, for eighty pounds. I was hard up at the time, and I had to sell a young horse from the farm before I could complete the purchase. For the first ten days after the bar re-opened the takings doubled. The customers were going round the town telling their friends of the horrible painting I had inflicted on them, so the friends came into the bar to see the painting for themselves. I still have it; Christie's valued it recently at five thousand pounds.

Another new interest for me was the management of the cellar. It was one more thing I knew nothing about — less than nothing, for I was teetotal. The cellar was poor — not good enough to cater for the level of customers we were attracting. Amongst the customers were representatives of some of the best of the London wholesale wine importers, who were travelling the country calling on the provincial wine merchants. Most of them were either directors or partners in their firms. One was Herbert Sichel, a director of the famous Bordeaux house of Sichel and Company. He was about my own age, and fortunately he was ready to help me. It was under his tutelage that I began my education in wine. Another wine man, Patrick Guimaraens, a director of Parrot and Company, was a great help to me. His firm imported Veuve Clicquot champagne, Liger Belair burgundy, and Fonseca port. Patrick remained a friend and collaborator throughout my hotel career. I found the study fascinating; it is a study that can never be completed; wine has such infinite variety. Gradually, with the help of Herbert Sichel, Patrick Guimaraens and others, the cellar was improved until in course of time it became one of the best features of the hotel.

Another interesting aspect of my new work was the preparation of the hotel literature: the booklets, the holiday leaflets and the wine list. Here again I owed a debt to Charles. He had discovered an exceptionally good printer, Harold Curwen of the Curwen Press, Plaistow. Curwen drew on the work of a group of young artists, such men as Barnet Freedman, Eric Ravilious and Edward Bawden, who were able to produce designs and layouts that expressed the character of the hotel.

I discovered Edward Bawden myself. I saw some illustrations of murals in the Illustrated London News which had been carried out by Bawden at Morley College. The principal subject was a lodging house with a classical pediment and with the front walls taken out, so that the life in the house was shown from the basement to the attic. I found it delightful. I managed to find out where he lived — Rembrandt Studios, Redcliffe Road, Earls Court — and I went to see him. I rang his bell; waiting on the steps I looked across the road and recognised the building that was the subject of the mural. At length a young and seemingly timid man came to the door; "There is your mural", I said. He told me that I was the first person to spot his subject. He took me on a bus to see the paintings on the walls of Morley College.

The outcome was that he designed a wine list for the hotel, decorated a large ordnance map of Scarborough (which when I left the hotel I gave to the children's public library) and also made an amusing perspective peep-show box, which is still in my possession. Later his friend Eric Ravilious, another young artist, designed and illustrated the hotel booklet, all the printing being done by Curwen.

It was Charles who had first adopted the policy of making use of artists. My contact with the artists, and my wider interest in art (generated and encouraged by Bruce Turner), grew until it became one of the principal interests in my life.

Although there was so much to occupy me at the hotel,

I had not cut myself off from my farming interests. Mr. Palfreyman, the tenant of one of my father's farms at Lockton, had retired and I took over the tenancy of his farm, so that I could retain some interest in farming. As Jim Ferguson, the shepherd at Hulam who lived in a tied cottage had reached retirement age, he was looking for somewhere to retire to. I offered to put him in charge of the farm and I gave him the opportunity to run it on pastoral lines, so that he could farm it with a stick and a dog. He accepted and he came down with his housekeeper bringing his dog, Jed, with him. The few acres of arable land were laid down to grass; and the farm was stocked with a flock of half-bred sheep, bred from Cheviot ewes by a border Leicester ram, also a herd of Galloway cows running with a white Shorthorn bull. I was adopting the hill farming system of the Northumberland moorland farms, for which the Lockton farm was suitable, and for which Jim Ferguson had the right experience.

The farm incorporated an extensive rough pasture of over one hundred acres, with good rough grazing, scrubland and sheltered woodlands; on the southern boundary was a moorland trout stream. Galloways are small shaggy black cattle, low to the ground, gentle, and extremely hardy. They settled down in the rough pasture and soon became acclimatised. They kept together in a herd except when a cow was coming on to calf, when she would disappear into the scrub, eventually re-appearing with her calf at foot. Crossed with a white Shorthorn bull, they produced calves with a blue-grey coat. In the summer the herd of Galloways was a most beautiful sight, the cows contented, the calves playful; I have never seen anything that has given me more satisfaction.

I kept on my father's shoot and even enlarged it by taking the Bridestones moor, a small grouse moor only two miles away from the farm. It was small but just the right size to be shot by two guns shooting over Pointer dogs.

Harland and I had about six days each season on the moor, which produced a total bag of about sixty brace of grouse. I preferred the grouse shooting to the mixed shooting over the small Lockton farms.

There is a freedom about a grouse moor, no cultivation, undisturbed nature, especially as we managed it with no grouse butts; we did very little heather burning yet the moor always seemed to be well stocked with birds.

Once we turned off the lane leading to the moor we found ourselves on sandy tracks which, on the Bridestones moor, are in part covered by pure silver sand. The scent of the heather, the call of the grouse, the sweep of the land with Blakey Topping in the distance and the magnificent Bridestones on the moor itself, made an exciting and deeply satisfying world.

Shooting over Pointers suited me. I would never have been able to hit driven grouse, but I did bring down birds flushed by the dogs although I was not a good shot. But I would often wound a bird instead of killing it outright. It was revolting having to kill a wounded grouse or a partridge before putting it into the shooting bag and gradually I turned against it. Harland had no such qualms. To him, shooting was a way of life and in any case he did not wound his birds, he killed them outright.

He had started his working life as a groom and had never lost his interest in horses. When he realised that I was losing interest in shooting, and knowing that I rode, he suggested that I should give up shooting and take up hunting. He pointed out that I could stable horses at the farm and that he could look after them. We looked round the farm buildings together. There was a two-horse stable with a loose box, and a place for a saddle room. I knew of a good jobbing joiner and he came to Lockton and did the necessary work. In the meantime, Harland looked out for two suitable hunters and when he found them we purchased them together.

Looking back, I regret the change. Although I was a bad shot, I enjoyed my shooting with Harland. Hunting was entirely different. In my experience the hunting field is as much a social activity as a sporting occasion. If I had my time over again I would persevere with shooting and leave the hunting field alone.

The master of our local pack of foxhounds was Jack Renwick, an impecunious racehorse trainer from the nearby market town of Malton. He was the image of Jorrocks, broad and plump with a shining red face and a hearty manner. He lived for horses and was a wonderful judge of anything on four legs. He found me useful, as he was often very hard up; he would come to the hotel to cash cheques, warning me that they would probably bounce, but promising to let me know when they could be re-presented. He was a reliable, unreliable man; his cheques did bounce, but he kept his word and we always got the money in the end. As he was such a rum character he was not popular in orthodox hunting circles, and his hounds had a poor following except amongst the small farmers and the sporting labourers. Harland did not approve of him — he thought him too free and easy.

Harland had a great respect for the gentry and he tried to educate me in their ways. He had little stories which illustrated how a gentleman should behave out in the hunting field, especially in a delicate situation. One of these ran as follows: "If you are out 'unting, Mr. Tom, and are riding home alongside a young lady after a long day in the field, should you pass a farmhouse say to the young lady: "Lady, would you like a glass of milk?".

Harland's thoughts turned naturally to women. He was a believer in courting. I happened to mention that I had been riding alongside an attractive young woman on a previous day's hunting. Harland's eyes lit up: "H'enjoy yourself whilst you are young, Mr. Tom, I always did, I never lost a h'opportunity". He would never elaborate and

I had to work out for myself what he meant by an "opportunity".

It was during my first few years back at home that the farm became the focal point for the family. My brother Frank, who was four years younger than I was, fell seriously ill with a tubercular spine which necessitated a very serious operation. After the operation he had to lie on a steel frame which held his spine in a rigid grip for months. He was brought back from the hospital to Lockton, where he was nursed back to health by my cousin, Mollie Nasbet, who was the same age as my brother Charles. Mother spent as much time as she could at Lockton and the family gathered round her.

All this activity was unexpected and too much for Jim Ferguson's housekeeper to cope with. He was offered a cottage in his native Scottish border country for his retirement, so we closed the farm, sold the cattle and sheep, and let the land, keeping on the farmhouse as a holiday residence.

Not long after Jim's departure Harland fell ill with cancer. I had never known him have a day's illness before. Although he was well on in his seventies, he had been able to outwalk and outride any one of us. He took to his bed and quickly wasted away almost to a skeleton, enduring the most terrible pain. One of the last times I saw him he said to me: "Mr. Tom, if I could get my gun I'd shoot myself". It was a sad end for a fine man.

After Harland's death I sent my horses to the Mill at Langtoft on the Yorkshire Wolds. It was a livery stables run by Cecil Jackson and his assistant, Roy Hey — both fine horsemen. The country was hunted by the Middleton East pack of hounds. The Master, Wickham Boynton, was a crack horseman, an intimidating, aristocratic type of man, a very different character from Jack Renwick. It was fine open rolling country, with light land and small hedges. I rode alongside Roy Hey, who rode straight whatever the type of hedge. We had some marvellous days together. Back at the hotel it was a great feeling, to have a hot bath after a day's hunting, followed by ham and eggs and a bottle of burgundy. Had I been an Eastern potentate, that would have been the moment to bring on the dancing girls.

I hunted for two seasons from the Mill at Langtoft, but after that I pack it in as I was becoming too occupied with developments in the hotel.

CHAPTER VI

WITH CHARLES IN LONDON

Apart from the farm, the only breaks I got from the hotel were the times that I spent with Charles in London. Charles had established himself in lodgings above a butcher's shop at the top end of Long Acre. His landlady, Mrs. Forscutt, was the widow of a London baker whose family had supplied muffins to Buckingham Palace for generations. The description of his address by Charles was: "On the left, by the liver". There was usually a bunch of livers and lights hanging beside the front door.

His lodgings were extremely comfortable. The Forscutt family must have been well established for centuries, for some of their furniture dated back to Stuart days. There was a suite of early walnut furniture, and one of the finest groups of Chelsea china figures I have ever seen. Mrs. Forscutt was interested in the stage; she liked to have a young actor as a lodger; one of her former lodgers had been Henry Ainley. A spare bedroom led out of Charles's bedroom; I was encouraged to make use of it, not only by Charles, but also by mother, who was concerned that we should keep in touch.

My first visit was to attend the R.A.D.A. public show in 1926, which was held in the St. James's Theatre. Charles, who had only been at the Academy for nine months, was several years older than most of the students. He stood out at the public show, appearing several times, and at the end of the show he was given the premier award, the Bancroft Gold Medal.

Two of the Academy professors had taken a marked interest in him — Alice Gachet, the professor of French drama, and Theodor Komisarjevsky whose subject was the Russian theatre. At the time of the public show Komisarjevsky was directing a season of Russian plays in the suburban Barnes theatre, and on his suggestion Paul Ridgeway, the producer, gave Charles his first contract which was for twelve months at a nominal salary.

Charles' first professional appearance on the stage was as the servant in *The Government Inspector* by Turgenev, in which Claude Rains was playing the lead. Charles asked me to come up to London for the first night. I arrived at Long Acre the night before, to find him in a state of nerves. On the day of the opening we had lunch at his lodgings and took the bus out to Barnes. We trudged the common together, speaking of anything but the theatre, until the time came for me to leave him at the stage door. It was agonising to watch his performance but a relief to see how well he played up to the splendid performance of Claude Rains, who was playing his master.

Charles and I had a mutual interest in art. My visits were an opportunity for me to follow up the growing interest implanted by Bruce Turner. Charles made a knowledgeable guide to the galleries, as, apart from his work, they were his principal interest. He spent all his spare time in the National Gallery, the British Museum, the Victoria and Albert, the Tate, and the Wallace. In each he had found works which he showed to me with enthusiasm. At every succeeding visit he had discovered something new which he would rush me off to see — the small statue of Socrates in the British Museum, the "Woman Bathing" by Rembrandt in the National Gallery, the Guardis in the Wallace and the wonderful collection at Kenwood.

On my return home, I would tell Bruce Turner of the marvellous things I had seen. He was pleased with my enthusiasm but he wanted me to get my appreciation into a more balanced perspective. He suggested that I should study the collection of Italian paintings in the National

Gallery. "Start with the primitives", he said, "and work through the collection in chronological order".

I did exactly as he had advised, starting with the primitives, and making my way steadily from the thirteenth to the sixteenth century. It was a wonderful experience. At each visit I was discovering new treasures, each new treasure a logical development from what had gone before. Now there were times when the boot was on the other foot — I was showing Charles my discoveries. We were both enchanted by Crivelli, and by the two "Agonies in the garden" by Bellini and Mantegna, which are still two of my favourite paintings. As I worked through the centuries I realised how logical the development of painting had been. There was no mystery; each master was a product of his own generation, building on the foundations laid by the masters who had preceded him. It was an intensive study, and my eye became attuned to looking at masterpieces. Although I cannot claim to have become an expert, I believe that during the years when I spent so much time in the galleries, I acquired an eye that responded to quality in painting.

It was not all simple. Because of what Bruce Turner had told me, I turned from the Italian school towards the great European painters of the nineteenth century, starting with Géricault and Delacroix, then on to Courbet, Manet, Monet, Cézanne, Gauguin and Van Gogh. The gap between their work and the work of the sixteenth century Italians was too much for me to bridge. At first I found their work meaningless. Bruce had spoken enthusiastically of the painting by Van Gogh of his bedroom at Arles, which is hung in the Tate. I made a special expedition to see it, full of expectation, but I was disappointed. I could see nothing in it. I returned again and again, not only to the Van Gogh, but also to the Manets, the Monets, the Gauguins and the Cézannes. It was a long time before the power and intensity of Van Gogh broke through to me, and before I

was able to appreciate the brilliance and subtlety of
Monet. The last of all to dawn on me was the work of
Cézanne.

It was an exciting time. Charles was happy, completely
obsessed by his work, encouraged by Alice Gachet and
Komisarjevsky, working on his own parts, studying voice
production, studying the performances of other actors in
the West End shows, and relaxing in the picture galleries.
I saw most of his performances at the Barnes theatre. The
one I liked best was Epihodoff — the callow young clerk in
The Cherry Orchard. The productions of Komisarjevsky
at the Barnes were based on the Russian productions of
the Stanislavsky theatre. The Tchekov plays were especially delightful, my first experience of really good
theatre.

Komisarjevsky was engaged by Ivor Novello to direct
the Hungarian play *Liliom* in which Novello was playing
the lead. On the recommendation of Komisarjevsky,
Novello engaged Charles to play the park of Ficksur, a
pick-pocket. Half-way through the rehearsals Novello decided that Charles would not do and he instructed Komisarjevsky to find someone else. Komisarjevsky, looking on
Charles as his protégé, told Novello that if Charles was replaced he would resign, with the result that Charles stayed.

Liliom was given a provincial tour before opening in
London; I saw it in Leeds. In a scene on a railway embank-
ment in which Charles appeared with Novello, Novello
had placed himself in the centre of the stage, facing the
audience, with a spotlight on his face. Charles was in the
shadow, off centre, with his back to the audience, and yet
he contrived to be convincing and effective. When the play
reached London the critics gave Novello bad notices, but
one famous critic picked out Charles, contrasting the
effectiveness of his realistic performance, with the un-
reality of Novello. Novello had been right; he had sensed
that the realism of Charles's performance was not a

foil to his own pseudo-romantic style.

During his second year Charles had several successes. He played an American in *The Happy Husband.* His American accent was so good that one of the critics thought that he was a young American actor new to the London stage. He had acquired the accent by studying a record of President Coolidge addressing a gathering of farmers.

This was followed by a success in *Mr. Prohack,* in which he played the lead: it was the play in which he met Elsa Lanchester. Soon after, Charles introduced me to Elsa — a remarkable young woman with lively brown eyes, hair the colour of burnished copper, an incisive voice, and a critical mind. She had been running a night club for years which she called "The Cave of Harmony". When I knew it, it was in Seven Dials, and it was the only non-commercial night-club I have known. Run by Elsa and her friends as a vehicle for their talents, it had wit and spontaneity, and the charges were ridiculously reasonable. The decorations were mostly done by a young painter, John Armstrong, who also seemed to have a lot to do with the catering. There was no licence and refreshments were served in a basement where I paid four pence for a kipper. I told Elsa that I thought it was too cheap. She was indignant. "They only cost two pence", she said, and with a piercing look, added, "We're not profiteers here, you know".

It was during this period that I saw at close quarters how Charles had to struggle to get himself into the skin of a part. He had to weigh up the mentality of the character he was playing, and start his mind working in the same direction. He was given the lead in a new play, *The Man with Red Hair,* adapted from a novel by Hugh Walpole.

There was time to take a holiday before rehearsals began, so we went together to the winter sports resort, Arosa. Mr. Crispin, the man with red hair, was a very unpleasant character, a wealthy dilettante, an art collector, and apparently a masochistic pervert. I found myself on the skiing slopes, accompanied by Charles who, obsessed with the part that lay ahead, was gradually transforming himself into a most peculiar type of man I was too inexperienced to understand. Charles conceived the idea that Mr. Crispin had in his make-up a good deal of the character of his creator, Hugh Walpole. On his return to London, he spent much time with Walpole studying him from every angle, even to the extent of finding out who made his clothes. It was a tailor in Savile Row, so Charles had his clothes for the part made by the same tailor; the only difference being that he asked him to exaggerate the style.

When the play opened, Charles' performance shocked and drew the town. It was so telling that the word went round that Charles himself was a pervert. During the run of the play I was dining at "The Basque Restaurant" in Dover Street when I heard an elderly gentleman at the next table blackguarding Charles, confusing his character with the character he was playing. I felt indignant, but on reflection I realised that it was unimportant; what did matter was that he had set the town talking.

Charles was still living in his lodgings at Long Acre. If I was with him when he was playing in the West End, we would walk together to the theatre, and I would leave him at the stage door. The streets in the West End, especially those in the theatre area, were full of prostitutes. Leaving the stage door, whichever way I went, were girls standing in doorways, walking in pairs on the pavements, and in groups at every street corner. They were unmistakeable, flashily dressed, heavily made up, smiling at the passing men and stopping to talk if a man showed the least interest. It was a horrible introduction to the practice of sex — furtive, sordid and sterile — until I met Madge.

CHAPTER VII

A FEW WILD OATS

I met Madge on the street just as I had met other prostitutes. She was young and nervous, walking the street with
another girl who was older and much tougher looking
than Madge. The tough girl who saw that I was attracted,
did all the talking, and the three of us went back to a
sleazy flat in Gloucester Road where Madge and I were
left together.

It would have been difficult for two people to have met
under more unpleasant circumstances and yet our meeting
was the start of a long, and at times a very happy relationship. We got on well not only physically but in every
other way.

Shortly after I met her, Charles left his lodgings in
Long Acre to marry Elsa, and to set up house in a flat in
Percy Street. I went to their wedding in a Registry Office
with Iris Barry, a friend of Elsa's, and from her asides to
me I gathered that she thought they were making a mis-
take. "It will have a ghastly effect on their Income Tax"
she said.

When I went up to London, after Charles and Elsa were
married, I stayed with Madge. She moved from the flat in
Gloucester Road to Museum Street, and soon after to a
flat in Conduit Street above an antiquarian bookseller.
When I let Madge know that I was coming, she cleared the
deck so that I could stay with her without interruption.
We lived together in her flat; went to shows and restaurants; we even spent hours together in the galleries and
museums.

We were an incongruous pair. Madge was tall and slender

with striking looks, and as she gradually became more prosperous she dressed beautifully. One day we were walking down Bond Street together and I noticed that men were turning round to stare at us. I asked Madge why. "Don't you know?" she said, "It's because I'm so smart and you're so shabby". Places like the Ritz frightened me, but she delighted in plunging me into such smart surroundings. I preferred the smaller places like the "Etoile" in Charlotte Street, or the "Eiffel Tower" in Percy Street, where the Rossi family and Stulik made their customers welcome, and where the surroundings were simpler and more congenial. For a time our favourite restaurant was the newly-opened "Boulestin" at the corner of Leicester Square and Panton Street, small, intimate, not over-decorated and serving genuine French cooking with a sound selection of French wines to choose from. The Diaghilev Russian Ballet Company was performing at the Coliseum Theatre, filling the second half of the programme. We dined at "Boulestin" and strolled to the theatre to arrive during the interval; the first time we were late. Entering the auditorium, the darkness, cut by the shafts of light from the limes shining down on the brilliant stage, was a wonderful experience. I had never known such a combination of movement, colour and music. Walking back through the West End to Madge's flat in Conduit Street we were transported, united by our enchantment. We became habitués, dining first at "Boulestin" and arriving at the theatre for the interval for as long as the ballet season lasted. When it closed we turned to the "Hungaria Restaurant" in Lower Regent Street, more for the Magyar music than for the food. Another restaurant we liked was the "Basque" in Dover Street, which was good but not as good as "Boulestin".

We spent our holidays together – the first in the spring-time at a rented Yorkshire farm-house in Farndale. I met Madge off the London train at York; she was curious to know where we were going. I told her it was to a primitive farm-house in a beautiful remote country valley. She was very practical; "I shall have to have a wedding ring", she said, "we will get one at Woolworth's". At the counter, trying on the ring, she happened to look at me and burst out laughing. She told me afterwards it was because I looked so guilty.

After Woolworth's we went to the market to buy goods, where we bought all kinds of nice things including some early green peas. When we got to the farm we found very few cooking utensils — it was so short of pots and pans that the peas had to be cooked in a kettle, and we had a job to get them out! The farm was not very comfortable but we had a lovely time. Farndale is so beautiful; the stream that runs down the valley is flanked with fields and banks covered with wild daffodils. We were gloriously happy there.

Later Madge heard of an exclusive hotel, the Formentor in Majorca, so we booked to go there. We travelled by train to Barcelona and we arrived in time to see the Queen of Spain being met from Madrid by a party of officials, all dressed in black. That evening Barcelona was seething with excitement; I had never seen such a gay city. We were sorry to have to embark on the ship for Palma.

The Formentor was a beautiful hotel, but we did not care for it. After a few days we took a boat and sailed round the promontory into Pollensa Bay, where we managed to rent a fisherman's cottage. Our landlady, Caterina, lived in the cottage next door. A fishing boat was being built just a few yards away, and we hired a sailing dinghy which was moored to a little jetty barely twenty yards from the cottage. We were surprised when, a few days after our arrival, everyone stopped work. Flags and bunting suddenly appeared all along the shore. "What is it?" I asked Caterina in my halting Spanish. "It is the Republic", she replied. We had lived through a revolution without knowing what was going on.

We took Caterina's cottage for two years running. In those days the development in Majorca had scarcely started and there had been no development at all in Pollensa Bay. We were very happy there, Madge doing the cooking and I doing the shopping. We brought supplies with us for our second visit so that we could entertain, having made friends amongst a small circle of English-speaking writers and painters who had settled there. Puerto Pollensa had been the holiday home of Sorolla, the Spanish painter. I came across a beautiful small painting of a Spanish working boy resting during the mid-day break. I had never heard of Sorolla, but I was lucky enough to recognise the quality of this painting and to acquire it.

We were so happy at Pollensa that we were tempted to settle there. We came across a dilapidated country house on the promontory of the magnificent land-locked bay. It would have made an hotel with ample room for terraced gardens, a swimming pool, and its own private beaches. Because of its situation there would always be cool sea breezes in the hot weather. We looked across the bay from our little jetty, and we played with the idea of buying it and setting up together as hotel-keepers. I sailed the little dinghy across the bay, found a landing place and got ashore. It was a delightful situation full of possibilities; looking back across the bay I saw the village church and I thought that we could be married there. It was only a thought; I had not the courage to break away from my responsibilities at home.

On the way back we spent a day in Barcelona, lunching at the "Colon" before taking the train for Paris. At the door of our railway carriage we found H.G. Wells saying goodbye to a lady who was travelling to Paris in the same carriage. H.G. Wells had been attending a literary conference in Barcelona. It looked as though he might have been improving the occasion by further exploration in the world of sex, and we guessed by his attitude that as far as he was concerned his latest exploration was over. As the train drew out he looked so relieved.

We stayed in Paris for a few days at the Continental Hotel, doing a round of the night clubs. Our favourite was the "Scherherazade" which was supposed to be run by White Russian emigré aristocrats. Whether they were or not, they had evolved a remarkable technique for taking your money, and at the same time preserving an attitude of aristocratic disdain. Leaving the club was a hazardous business. A ragged old lady sat in the porch selling beautiful white lilac, the most expensive lilac in Paris. The be-medalled doorman summoned a taxi — an ancient Rolls Royce driven by a chauffeur dressed as a Russian cavalry officer. The combination of the Rolls and its disdainful aristocratic driver required a gratuity of no ordinary dimensions.

I arrived back home a shaken man. Madge sent me a paper-thin platinum dress watch, by Cartier of Paris, as a memento of the occasion. The letters "T.C.F." were inscribed on the back. Madge refused to explain them. It was stolen a few years ago. The traffic was not all one way. Madge would sometimes come to Scarborough, staying at the Pavilion. She insisted that she should remain incognito, and not be introduced to the family. I suspect, however, that they knew what was going on. Mother did not say a word — it was not her practice to remonstrate with us. She was a great one for prayers, which I believe were in the long run more effective than any remonstration.

One day I received a letter from Madge telling me that she was going to be married. I was stunned. I rushed up to mother to tell her that I must go to London. Mother saw in my hand the letter with the familiar hand-writing. "All right, Tom", she said. "Go, but for God's sake be careful". I did not have the chance to be anything else. On my arrival in London I telephoned Madge. She would not see me.

CHAPTER VIII

HOLBECK HALL

With Madge lost to me, Charles married, and my horses sold, there was nothing left to distract me from my work in the hotel. It was doing well, but the changing character of the business involved changes in the organisation. It was no longer an hotel in which men were in the ascendant, rather the reverse; to hold the business it was necessary to pay more attention to feminine taste.

There were only two bars, one catering for the general public who entered from the main street and one in the hotel itself, a smoke-room bar catering for men only. There was a need for a bar catering for both sexes. I thought of John Armstrong, who had carried out the decorations for Elsa's "Cave of Harmony". I explained to John that I wanted a bar that would provide a becoming setting for women, that would add to the social life of the hotel, and be situated in proximity to the ballroom. He accepted my commission to design and carry out the décor. At the time chromium plate and shining mirrors were in fashion; John did not like chromium, so he decided to base his scheme on polished pewter and rose-tinted mirrors — an altogether softer combination.

He designed the bar, and when the structural part was completed he came to Scarborough to decorate the walls with murals which he painted himself. He was a striking looking man, tall, slim and ascetic. He had uniquely individual taste, which showed in his dress and in everything he did. His most characteristic feature was a very special sense of humour.

He did the murals at night, locking himself in the bar.

All that he asked was that we should not look in until his work was finished and that we should keep him supplied with bottled Guinness. It took him three nights and three cases of Guinness. The finished bar was most attractive, and immediately successful; it became the social meeting place for the district, and was a great asset to the hotel dances. Following the bar, I commissioned John to decorate the ballroom suite; his completed work added considerably to the distinction of the hotel.

Nevertheless, with all the changes, it was still essentially a family hotel. The words conjure up a rather sticky sort of establishment, but nothing could be further from the reality. The Pavilion was attracting very bright families, amongst them some extremely attractive daughters, who in their turn were attracting some very bright young men. They were coming so regularly that they constituted a Pavilion set, so that the hotel had the atmosphere of a social club, the members of which arrived confident that they were going to enjoy themselves.

The highlights of the Pavilion seasons were provided by the ballroom fetes. I have not spent a great deal of time in night clubs, but I have never come across one so gay as the gala nights at the Pavilion. The dancing stopped at 1.30 a.m. but the parties ran on for hours after the dancing was over. Bottle after bottle of champagne was consumed, magnums became a commonplace, they even graduated as far as Jeroboams. Not all the young men were staying in the hotel; some would mysteriously fade away in the small hours of the morning and it was many years afterwards that I discovered where they went to. The railway station was opposite the hotel; some of the younger and more impecunious members of the set had sufficient money to stand their corner at the parties, but not enough to do that and to pay their hotel bill. They solved the problem by bedding down in the empty carriages standing in the railway sidings opposite the hotel.

It was mother who kept the hotel on an even keel. Her presence was its greatest asset. She had founded the business, and during her long career she had built up a reputation and earned affection from a very wide circle. The older she got the more distinguished she became, and the more her presence in the hotel was appreciated; a word from her would quell the most rowdy of our customers.

By now my brother Frank was sufficiently recovered from his operation to leave the farm at Lockton and come back to the hotel. He was still delicate and temperamentally shy, but behind his shy exterior there was a toughness and determination that enabled him to master anything in which he was interested.

When he came back from the farm he interested himself in the technical work at the back of the hotel. He spent hours in the cabinet maker's workshop and the laundry, but his principal interest was in the kitchens. From childhood he had been interested in cooking, and one of his playgrounds had been in the kitchens with the chefs. When he was a very little boy someone had bought him a chef's outfit — blue and white check trousers, a double-breasted white jacket, a white neckerchief, and a tall white hat. He loved to be in the kitchen, dressed like the other chefs, carrying out the simple jobs they gave him. It was only play, but it laid the foundation for his career as an outstanding restaurateur.

We worked well together, but I realised that there would not be sufficient scope in the hotel for both of us, so I started to look round for a property in which we could expand. It had to be something local, as at this stage Frank was not robust enough to be left on his own. The Pavilion was in the centre of the town. I would have liked an hotel on the sea front, but none was available. However, there was a fine property on the southern end of the Esplanade; a large house on the edge of the cliff surrounded by a few acres of garden, with no public road between it and the sea. We bought it and I set about conversion.

Making it into a country house type of hotel took two years, and when it was completed we named it Holbeck Hall. At that time my mother's younger sister, Winifred Goodman, was managing the Golf Hotel in Marienbad, a small exclusive establishment about the same size as Holbeck Hall. She was wanting to come back to England, so she returned to Scarborough to take over the new hotel. We knew her as "Auntie Winnie". She was very feminine, with attractive looks, a charming personality and a style of her own. She soon settled down and enjoyed building up a new clientele, running the hotel successfully with little trouble to us.

I then found myself looking for something else. Although we were doing well, we were not making a great deal of money, mainly due to my lack of business training and knowledge of accountancy. I did not realise the need to budget ahead, to provide for depreciation, repairs, renewals, and for development; with the result that if we were to expand, I had to find someone to finance us. The only source I knew of was the bank. We banked at a small branch in Falsgrave with a meticulous manager, who, I felt, did not approve of me. He knew I was casting around looking for some field in which to expand, and he also knew that we had very little cash. What cash we had, had gone into the development of the Holbeck Hall Hotel.

Our accountants were a Sheffield firm. Mr. Toplis, the partner who looked after our affairs, told me that the company owning the Grand Hotel in Sheffield was in difficulties, and that it was looking for additional capital and new management. He asked me whether I would be interested. A disadvantage of our business in Scarborough was its seasonal character. It seemed to me that a provincial city hotel would have a better all-the-year round type of trade, and that its quiet season would coincide with our busy season, so I started to investigate.

The question was, would our bank finance me? I did not feel that I could discuss the matter with the bank manager; I was certain that he would disapprove. I did not tell him what I had in mind, I just asked him to make an appointment for me at the bank's head office in London.

In the meantime the negotiations progressed. The accountants who were controlling the company changed their attitude; they decided that rather than go for a reconstruction they would sell the company outright. The Grand was in those days the largest hotel in Sheffield, standing on a central site which included vacant land that would allow for expansion. It had restaurants, banqueting rooms and bars, but it was in a run-down state and losing money. After protracted bargaining, the company was offered to us for seventy thousand pounds. The assets included the freehold site, and the hotel, complete with all its furnishings, equipment and stocks.

Meanwhile my bank manager had made no appointment for me at head office. It was now urgent; I told him that I was going down to head office and that I should see someone, even if he was only the door-keeper. That produced results; when I did go I had an appointment with one of the general managers.

It was my first experience of the City. The general manager's office was large and imposing, making me feel very inadequate, which indeed I was. With my lack of accounting knowledge I should have had our accountant to help me. Without him I had to make my case as best I could. The general manager listened with close attention to what I had to say; some way through the interview a bank messenger came into the room and handed him a slip of paper. I wondered what on earth it could be — something important judging by the attention he gave it. He looked up from the paper, and with a smile gave me the latest Test Match score! He seemed more interested in me than in the particulars of the hotel that I was asking him to finance. He wanted to know my background, my attitude to hotel keeping, why I wanted to expand, why I wanted to buy a provincial city hotel, and if it was bought how I intended to develop it. It was fortunate for me, for if it had been mainly a question of figures, I should have been hopelessly unprepared. At length he seemed satisfied. I was asking the bank to advance seventy thousand pounds on the security of our property in Scarborough, and on the hotel I was going to purchase. He told me that the bank would be prepared to advance the money, but that the transaction must be arranged through the usual channel. He explained; "You must discuss the matter with your bank manager, and he will make the arrangements". The idea of discussing it with my disapproving manager seemed impossible to me. I had hesitated to tell him what I was thinking about; I could not imagine myself telling him that I wanted to borrow seventy thousand pounds. I tried to explain, but the general manager was adamant. I came away with the assurance that the money would be forthcoming, but feeling very uneasy about having to explain myself to the local bank manager.

On the way home I spent the night in Sheffield staying at the Grand Hotel. I was joined in the bar by Toplis, who introduced me to the regional manager of Barclay's Bank, telling him that I was negotiating to buy the hotel. The regional manager asked me whether I had got the money. I told him of my position – he offered to look into it, and he invited me to have dinner with him. Over dinner he showed how well he understood the situation. He knew the Grand Hotel well, how badly it required new management; he also knew the Pavilion Hotel at Scarborough. He thought that our proposed purchase was a sound proposition, and he offered to go to London on the following morning to discuss the matter at his head office. He promised to telephone me by mid-day to tell me what his bank would be prepared to do. When he did telephone, it was to tell me that his bank was prepared to finance the deal to the extent of providing eighty thousand pounds on the security that I was offering. With this offer there was no need for any further negotiations with a local bank manager, so with his assurance, Toplis and I went to Leeds where the negotiations had been taking place. The deal was closed, and the hotel bought subject to the approval of my brother Frank.

Frank had been following the negotiations with the feeling that nothing would come of them owing to the difficulty of finance. When I arrived back home with the news that the deal was completed, he was shocked. He found it difficult to realise that the finance was arranged and he was frightened by the obligations it involved. He asked me who would run the hotel in Sheffield. I thought he had understood it would be me, and when I told him he became distressed. He felt he was not yet capable of being left on his own. The more we discussed it, the more determined he became not to agree. I had made the deal subject to his approval, so in the end I gave in, and I wrote to withdraw.

It was a disappointment, but it was just as well. It probably saved me from becoming a manipulator of hotels rather than being a straightforward hotel-keeper. At the time it left me with no other course but to continue my education in the hotel business at home in the Pavilion. I could not have had a better school, my teachers being the team of experienced staff many of whom I had grown up with. Chef Moore, Heseltine and later Gibson — the two head waiters; Driscoll and Henderson — the lounge and wine waiters; Albert and Arthur Midgeley — the cellarmen; Miss Thwaites, the receptionist; Miss Turner, the book-keeper; Mrs. Reeve, the cashier and control clerk; Hilda West, the storekeeper; Vera Hick, the head stillroom maid; Doris and Kathleen, the men's smoke-room barmaids; Fred

King in charge of the new American bar; Arthur Drysdale, Bob Moore and George Pottage, the porters; Miss Tibbs — the housekeeper, Shepherd, the maintenance joiner and cabinet-maker, a team of excellent waitresses headed by Edith Grant and Nora Lishman, and an equally good team of chambermaids headed by Grace Gibson. Every single one of them was a person of quality and some of them had been at the hotel as long as I could remember. Between them all, they had created a remarkable hotel.

The lesson to be learnt at the Pavilion was the value of service; it was there at every corner of the hotel. From the business angle my lack of accountancy training was the principal weakness. All my attention was given to running the hotel as well as I could, without much thought as to the financial outcome. I played a considerable part in adding to the interior of the hotel by my co-operation with John Hill, the decorator, and by this time my collection of paintings was becoming a feature. My main attention was given to the catering. Most of the guests stayed at the hotel on inclusive terms, which covered their bedroom and four meals a day. These consisted of a four-course breakfast, a five-course lunch, a substantial afternoon tea, and a six-course dinner. And this was provided at charges ranging from seventy-five pence to one hundred and twenty-five pence per day, with no additional charge for service.

It was a constant struggle keeping the meals interesting and avoiding too much repetition. There was no difficulty with the breakfasts or the afternoon teas, and not a great deal with the luncheons. There is such a wide range of splendid English dishes for lunch, so good that they will bear fairly frequent repetition. English luncheons with our excellent soups, broths, fish, our splendid meat, our extensive range of puddings, tarts and other sweets are unequalled in the world. In England because of the fine meat, the roast cook is as important as the sauce cook. In

France a good roast cook is a rarity. That is one of the reasons why, on balance, I prefer English food to French.

At the hotel it was the evening dinner menus that were the most difficult to compose. To keep them interesting and varied it was necessary to make use of the classical French dishes. I found the study of Saulnier's "Repertoire de la cuisine Francaise" and Escoffier's "Le Guide Culinaire" an indispensable aid. I do not care for the use of the French language in the composition of menus in English hotels, but when it comes to composing dinner menus stretching over a period of three to four weeks, it is impossible to avoid it. That is what we had to do, as many of our customers would stay for up to four weeks. We tried to present them with a repertoire of menus over the period with as little repetition as possible – no easy task.

Staying at the Pavilion was a gastronomic marathon to which the bulk of the customers stood up manfully, but there were casualties. It was not uncommon for a customer to retire to bed on the third or fourth day temporarily defeated. The hotel doctor knew how to cope, his usual prescription was a couple of days in bed on a light diet, which we were accustomed to providing.

CHAPTER IX

TUNING UP FOR TUNNY ·

As far as I was concerned, the few years after my abortive attempt to buy the Grand Hotel at Sheffield were the easiest and most carefree period of my hotel life. With my horses sold, I took up swimming for exercise and bathed in the sea every day throughout the year. One wintry morning there was an icy wind lifting the sand and sending it scudding along the shore. When I came out of the sea the icy sand stuck to my wet skin, turning me into a piece of living sandpaper. The pain of trying to dry myself and remove the sand was excruciating. After that I confined my bathing to the summer months.

In the winter I explored the country that lies behind Scarborough. Every Sunday I walked from twenty to thirty miles, exploring the dales, the moorlands and the cliffs. It was a wonderful experience and I came to realise more fully what a magnificent part of the world I lived in.

During the summer I had a swimming partner, a beautiful young girl called Isobel Hepworth. She was a superb swimmer and she would have made a perfect model for a Maillol sculpture. She was eight years younger than I. Her parents had a holiday residence in Scarborough and when they came we bathed together every day. We started the sport of aquaplaning, which was such a novelty in Scarborough that we were asked to give a demonstration in the course of one of the regattas. We aquaplaned together backwards and forwards around a crowded Marine Drive at the foot of the Castle Hill.

It was during this period that a new sport came to Scarborough — ·fishing for tunny. The originator in

Scarborough was a noted big-game angler, Mitchell Henry, who was a guest at the Pavilion; he sailed for the fishing grounds from Scarborough harbour. He caught his first tunny towards the end of August 1930; it weighed five hundred and sixty pounds, and before the end of the season four more were landed including one of seven hundred and thirty pounds.

The following year several other sportsmen came after the tunny; amongst them was Lord Egerton, who stayed at the Pavilion. He stayed for two years running without catching a fish until towards the end of his third visit he landed two. He was a very quiet, unobtrusive man, and the day he landed the two fish he was dining by himself, so I went to his table to congratulate him. He was treating himself to an especially good bottle of claret, and he asked me to join him. "Sit down, Laughton", he said, "I will tell you about it". "Do you know", he went on, "this is a wonderful moment for me. I have had a dreadful time, I hate the sea, I am a shockingly bad sailor, but I had to have a tunny for my big game museum. Thank God I have got one at last — you will never see me again". And we never did.

Harold Hardy, of the famous firm Hardy Brothers of Alnwick, the angling specialists, was one of the tunny angling guests. His firm made the tunny gear, and he brought a stock of elaborate and expensive tackle with him. He suggested that I should have a try, so eventually I decided that I would. The kit consisted of: a deep sea Zane Grey angling rod with a detachable butt, a reel with a capstan brake that would take five hundred yards of fifty-two thread line, a special seat with a socket to hold the butt of the rod, a canvas webb shoulder harness, a large gaff with a detachable head, spools of fifty-two thread line, and a supply of fifteen feet wire traces and five-inch hooks. Everything was designed to cope with the heavy strains that it had to stand up to.

I charted one of the local decked herring cobbles, the *Our Maggie*, skippered by Tom Pashby with a crew of three, and also a small dinghy with a boatman. The fishing is done from the small row-boat, which is carried on the deck or towed astern according to the weather.

Tunny follow the herring shoals. They are found alongside the herring drifters hauling their nets, and also following the trawlers when they are fishing in the vicinity of the herring. They are usually caught in the evening light and at dawn, but on a grey day at any time of the day. When the angler leaves the harbour he makes for the herring fleet and for the trawlers fishing in the vicinity. The drill is to leave the harbour at high tide sometime before midnight, and to arrive at the herring fleet in time for the hauling of the nets at dawn. If there are tunny about, the angler gets into the small rowing-boat with his boatman, wearing his harness, holding the rod at the ready, the hook baited with a herring. Herrings are thrown round about the baited hook to attract the tunny as they scavenge the herrings round about the nets. If they are there, there is usually a small shoal of from four fish upwards. The herrings are taken readily, including, if all goes well, the baited hook.

That is the theory. My charter of the *Our Maggie* was for four weeks. For the first three weeks we ranged the North Sea in the vicinity of the herring fleet without seeing a sign of a tunny. It was an interesting new experience, leaving the harbour, setting a northerly course past the Scarborough Castle Hill, with the lights of the town receding in the distance. Then, as it grew colder, going below into the smelly cabin with its small, glowing stove, having a cup of strong "char" made with condensed milk, and gradually getting to know the crew who were a sturdy lot, full of fun, and just as keen as I was to get a tunny.

It was a long hunt, and we saw many big fish; porpoises,

sharks, whales, but not a glimpse of a tunny. We became
friendly with some of the drifter skippers — mostly Scotsmen or Dutchmen — and with the skippers of the four
battered old trawlers that fished from Scarborough harbour, and always seemed to be in our neighbourhood. One
of the trawlers was skippered by Billie Normandale, a
plump little man who wore a bowler hat green with age,
and whose hail came over the water in the form of a
magnified "ginny" whisper.

One evening during the fourth week of the charter we
left the harbour about 7.30 p.m. making for the herring
fleet. About fifteen miles north-east of Scarborough we
came across Billie's trawler hauling the trawl at a steady
three to four knots. Tom Pashby set the course of the
Our Maggie alongside, at a distance of about twenty-five
yards. He gave the usual hail, "Any tunny?" Out popped
Billie's head from the wheel-house, "Yes", came his
unexpected reply, "They're following us". "When are you
hauling?" called Tom. "In about half an hour", replied
Billie.

I put on my shoulder harness, checked my gear, and
Tom baited the five-inch hook with a herring. Charlie the
row-boat man pulled the dinghy up, which was towing
astern. Whilst this was going on Tom gave a shout — he had
seen the black dorsal fin of a tunny cutting the surface of
the water between the two boats. I got into the dinghy in
time for the hauling of the trawl, and Charlie rowed our
little boat close to where the trawl net would break the
surface. As the trawl net neared the surface, the water
round us was broken by the fins and backs of the huge
tunny, frantically scavenging the fish falling out of the net.

My baited hook was dangling fifteen feet or so beneath
the surface. Suddenly there was a terrific pull, the top of
the rod shuddered, and for a moment the pressure nearly
brought it down to the dinghy thwarts. The reel brake was
lightly set, the line ran out at a frantic speed; all I could do

was to keep the point of the rod up, whilst Charlie rowed the boat in the direction the fish was going, to relieve the tension, and to give me the opportunity gradually to tighten the reel brake, until at length the fish was towing the boat. Then the line went dead. I started to reel in feeling I'd lost him. I was almost relieved but it was still there and off it went again.

It was dusk when the fish took. We had been towed away from the trawler and the *Our Maggie*. Charlie called out to me "Where's Tom? I can't see them, we're lost". We were on our own, in the mist and without a lantern in our boat. It took me nearly four hours to bring that fish to the gaff and most of the time we were lost to the *Our Maggie*. By the time Tom found us I was completely exhausted. I wanted Charlie to give me a knife to cut the line, but he wouldn't. All he would say was "Hang on, hang on". My arms were done, my back was aching with the strain of the harness. I could scarcely keep up the point of the rod, but I had got most of the line back again, and the fish was swimming in a circle about thirty yards from the dinghy. I had a flask of brandy aboard the *Our Maggie*. Tom managed to toss it into the dinghy. With the help of the brandy I got the steel trace to the top of the road, and Charlie managed to gaff the fish. We got a rope round its tail some time between 1.30 a.m. and 2 a.m. and we were back in Scarborough harbour shortly after dawn with the 600 lb. fish aboard. It was only two days before the end of the four weeks' charter.

CHAPTER X

MOVE TO THE ROYAL

The next three years were to be trouble free, with little else for me to do other than to consolidate my grip on the hotel business, and to enjoy the pleasure of operating a well run successful family hotel. Although it was running smoothly it was never dull. The changing pattern of the guests was constantly interesting, and by this time many of them were friends, and almost all were appreciative.

There is a similarity between the life of an actor and the life of an hotel-keeper. The actor depends on earning applause, the hotel-keeper on earning appreciation. The actor's applause is given in the mass, appreciation for the hotel-keeper is given individually. That applies more to the hotel proprietor than to the hotel manager. The latter is in a different position, having first to earn the appreciation of his financial masters and this can make the hotel guests his secondary consideration.

I was enjoying the life in the hotel every bit as much as the guests. In one respect I was in a position similar to that of an unmarried curate of a fashionable church who attracts the notice of the young ladies of his congregation. To them he appears a glamorous figure, a captive Sir Galahad, the dulcet tones of the church organ providing a heady background. The young lady guests at the Pavilion did not attend as regularly as the church-goers, and the character of the music in the hotel was different from the music of the church, but it had a similar effect. Like the curate I was a fixture, and I came in for a certain amount of attention.

It was bad for me. I don't think I realised that it was

merely because I happened to be convenient. Harland's words spoken at Lockton came back to me: "Enjoy yourself whilst you are young, Mr. Tom, I always did, I never lost an opportunity". I did my best to live up to his precept.

The success of the hotel was in no way comparable to the success that Charles was having on the stage. By this time, he had graduated from a leading actor on the London stage to a world-famous film star. The film that put him in the world class was *The Private Life of Henry VIII*, which was made in England. In it, his performance as King Henry brought Holbein's portrait to life and was a worldwide success.

Despite his great success, Charles still had a thought for me. He knew that I needed room to expand, and he thought it would be better for me to leave Scarborough. His first suggestion was that we should develop an hotel in Stratford-on-Avon. We went there together, but about the time we were considering it the question of taking over the Grand Hotel, Sheffield, cropped up and he agreed that it should be bought. His concern seemed to be to get me out of Scarborough. As he had escaped he seemed to think that I should do the same. The difficulty was my brother Frank; he was delicate and he showed no signs of getting married and setting up for himself. He wanted me to stay in Scarborough, which I was prepared to do, provided I could find something to give me more scope.

The opportunity came in 1935. The Royal Hotel on the Scarborough sea front came up for sale. It was a strange hotel, built in the early nineteenth century, one of the first large hotels to be built in the north of England. Many years ago it had been fashionable and successful, but now it was run down, dilapidated, and doing very little business. Not a very attractive proposition, except that it was more than twice the size of the Pavilion and would certainly keep me busy. So we bought it, together with a delightful little

Regency property immediately adjoining, in which I set up house. It was a daunting moment walking into the Royal to take over. I had left behind an hotel in almost perfect order with a loyal and experienced staff, and loyal and faithful customers, to arrive at an hotel shabby and down at heel, with scarcely any customers, and practically no experienced staff. One exception was Tom Conlin, the hall porter. He was nearly eighty years of age but still sprightly, and he had been at the Royal for over fifty years, seeing managements come and go. I couldn't help wondering whether he would see me join the procession of the defeated.

Another exception was the head of the kitchens, Chef Tognoli. Upon my arrival in the hotel, my first call was to the kitchens. The Royal had a poor reputation for food, so I was surprised to find that the chef appeared to be a good type of man. He showed me round the kitchens which were spacious but poorly equipped. An interesting feature was a built-in spit roast, with a deep shallow wall fire grate and a chain gear mounted on the wall above. It had been out of use for a long time, but it gave the kitchen an air of distinction. The main kitchen with its communicating larders, pastry kitchen, vegetable section, and pan room, was well laid out; but the stoves were almost dropping to pieces, and the stock of copper pans was practically non-existent. The chef showed me his stores — the stock was pitifully inadequate.

I told the chef that it was my practice to do the buying; he seemed pleased. I made it my first job to get the stores stocked with the basic materials required, and the second to order a battery of copper pans from our London suppliers; but apart from that, I left the chef alone to conduct his department. The food he produced seemed good to me, and the few customers there were kept saying how much it had improved.

When I first met him, Chef Tognoli was a lonely, taciturn

man, but he gradually opened out. He had had a varied career, starting as an apprentice chef in Florence, working for a time as a commis chef in Nice, than as a departmental chef in Genoa and Rome. At one time he had been chef to one of the Italian dukes. I had no experience of Italian food, so I arranged that once a week he should cook me a dinner delving back into his experience. It was illuminating.

He made good soufflés, including a wonderful fish soufflé made from the flesh of Dover sole pounded in a mortar, and served with lobster sauce. He distilled his own liqueurs and used them to flavour water and biscuit ices; but best of all he made delicious consommé. I only found out about his consommé after I had ordered stock pots and stands, including one especially for consommé. His consommé had a rich golden colour with the most delicious aroma, and the flavour matched the aroma. I asked him where he had learnt to make the consommé, and he told me he had served as a commis to the soup chef at the Hotel Negresco, Nice, in the days when it was one of the best hotels in Europe.

When the Royal closed down after the season, Chef Tognoli went to spend the winter at his home in the hills above the Italian lakes. He had told me of the vineyards round his native village, so I arranged that he should buy a couple of casks of wine on my behalf and send them back to the Royal. It proved to be a good coarse wine, excellent for cooking and good for Tognoli himself. He drank a bottle every day with his main meal. It did him good and helped him to keep going for a year or two longer.

My Harcourt Place house adjoining the hotel came into its own when the hotel closed down for the winter. It was a delightful little house with an unusual entrance leading out of a covered archway. It had a curved staircase from the entrance up to the first floor, the staircase being lit by a Georgian fan-light over the door; and it had a Georgian roof-light over the third floor. It was said to have been the summer residence of the original Mr. Debenham, of Debenham and Freebody, who came to Scarborough to supervise Marshall and Snelgrove in St. Nicholas Street (less than two hundred yards from Harcourt Place), which, in his day, was the most fashionable drapers' shop in the north of England.

Having my own front door, I was able to live in absolute privacy with my books, pictures and gramophone records, and it was a new experience having someone to look after me. Winnie Harrington, the chambermaid, who had left the Pavilion after my father's death, came back to be my housekeeper at Harcourt Place. Having known Winnie since my early childhood, it was delightful to have her back again. She knew that I had been very close to my father and she had agreed readily to return to look after me. She soon made the house into a home and we settled down together.

During the summer my architect friend, Harry Johnson, had adapted the house for my use. One of the rooms was converted into a library and music room in which there was a Bluthner grand piano, a gramophone with a huge gaping horn growing out of a swan-like neck, and a library of records that I had gathered with the guidance of a young musician friend, Eric Fenby. The main decoration in the music room (apart from the grand piano, the gramophone and the books) was a very large drawing by Bruce Turner, which seemed to symbolise the struggles and sufferings of men; it was very appropriate to my situation at the Royal. Bruce came to stay with me for an extended period, and Eric would often join us for the evenings which were mostly spent in the music room.

I had known Eric Fenby for a good many years. When first I met him he was a church organist and a relief organist at the Futurist cinema. He was thoughtful and sensitive, with an explosive enthusiasm which kept him always on the boil. He was my only musical friend. Like Bruce Turner with his knowledge of art, Eric's knowledge of music was far beyond my capacity to understand. Some time after I first knew him, he had been summoned by Delius to his home at Grez-sur-Loing, where he had become his musical amanuensis. He had established an extraordinary rapport, despite the crippled and distressed condition of Delius. The association had resulted in the publication of much magnificent music which otherwise would have been lost to the world. The association had been uniquely successful, but it had left Eric mentally and physically exhausted. He had spent most of the summer staying at our farm at Lockton, where I would go to join him whenever I could, usually for a walk over the moors.

On one of these walks, I was singing "On Ilkla Moor Baht 'at", again and again, no doubt untunefully – ad nauseam as far as Eric was concerned. There was competition; Eric began to sing "Ilkla Moor" but in a strangely foreign idiom. "What's that?" I asked him. "Ilkla Moor as Rossini would have written it", he replied. "What a marvellous idea, could you make it into an orchestral piece?" I asked. "Of course", he said, "no trouble at all".

Kneale Kelly, the conductor of the Scarborough Spa Orchestra, was staying at the Royal, so I put the idea to him, suggesting that he should feature it and ask Eric to conduct. The Scarborough Cricket Festival was approaching, at which there was to be a gala orchestral concert. Kneale Kelly adopted the idea, and issued posters featuring the new work, "Rossini on Ilkla Moor" by Eric Fenby, conducted by the composer.

It was done so quickly that I omitted to tell Eric. He came in from Lockton to go the the Cricket Festival and was confronted by the poster. He rushed in to see me. "Are you mad?" he asked, "How can I compose a piece in time for a performance next week?" "Well", I replied, "you told me it would be easy, in any case you have got it half composed already". The outcome was that he came to Harcourt Place and in my music room "Rossini on Ilkla Moor" took shape on paper. It proved to be a sparkling piece; Eric received an ovation, and more important the piece was performed over ninety times by various orchestras in the following year, and it is to be heard to this day.

I had a splendid winter. I was enjoying my freedom and enjoying battling with the problem of how to transform the hotel. I discussed my ideas with Charles, who suggested that I should use Wells Coates as my architect. Wells Coates had worked for him in converting the three top floors of a house in Gordon Square for his London home. It was a very successful conversion but mostly, I thought, due to Charles. The décor was austere, but it included a magnificent Renoir "The Judgement of Paris" which Charles had bought from Dr. Barnes, the collector from Philadelphia. This painting was in the living room, which was divided from the dining room and library by a pair of sliding doors decorated by John Armstrong with motifs of tropical animals, plants and flowers. Wells Coates, although a fashionable and successful architect, had been malleable and docile with the eminent Charles. I feared he would be very different with me, so I decided against him. Instead I worked with Harry Johnson, who was nearer my own age, and who I knew by experience was ready to assimilate my ideas.

I was able to give Harry a firm brief. I wanted to increase the sleeping capacity of the hotel from one hundred and eighty persons to two hundred and sixty and at the same time enlarge the dining room, lounges, ballroom and bars, to cater for that number. The existing hotel was spacious enough to allow this to be done. I calculated that the increased capacity of the hotel would add to the profitability, and consequently I was confident that the bank would provide the finance.

This was as far as I could go at the time as I had arranged with Herbert Sichel, the wine shipper, to sail to the United States in the *Normandie* to attend Herbert's wedding. We were to sail in November.

CHAPTER XI

TRIP TO AMERICA

The sea voyage to America was enjoyable; the quality of the food in the ship was superb. The foie gras, the smoked salmon, the consommé, the sauces, everything spoke of a kitchen run on lavish lines. I had an introduction to the chef, who invited me to have coffee with him in the galley and afterwards he showed me round.

He was an impressive man, courteous, confident and proud in his spotless chef's clothes, crowned by a tall chef's hat. I have never seen finer stoves or such a lavish battery of copper utensils as he showed to me in the galley, but the most impressive feature of all was the brigade of chefs covering every department. The larders were stocked with the best quality meat, fish and poultry; I noticed turbots, halibuts, Dover soles, salmon and sea trout, lobsters, scallops, mussels and oysters. It was a most comprehensive selection of fine quality food and all of it the produce of France. There was a fruit store with melons, muscat grapes, peaches, figs, apples — every sort of fruit one could think of. The kitchens and restaurants in the *Normandie* were a demonstration that France was the leading gastronomic country in the world.

The voyage ended only too quickly. When we landed I stayed on in New York for a few days, Herbert going straight to Cleveland. I stayed at the St. Regis Hotel, which was very good. I saw as much as I could of the other New York hotels and for the first time came across the phenomenon of the American business conference. During a six-weeks' stay, covering a number of cities, it became apparent that the conference business was one of the mainstays of the American hotel trade. The conference delegates milled about in the public rooms, rushing from meetings to cocktail parties, in and out of trade displays in private rooms (almost always with a private bar attached), gathering for huge lunches, elaborate dinners and cabarets. All this was going on not only in New York but in almost every city I visited. It was something that I had not seen in England. I wrote to Harry Johnson, the architect, describing what I was seeing. By now, I had the idea that the plans for the Royal should be adapted so that we could cater for this type of business.

The investigations of the American hotel scene were incidental to the main purpose of my visit which was to stand by Herbert Sichel during his wedding celebrations. At Cleveland, I was the guest of Leonard Hannah in a mansion on the main Cleveland boulevard. Herbert was marrying Peggy Heaton. The Heatons were a wealthy family of manufacturers, with a circle of rich friends, including my host, Leonard Hannah. Leonard's mansion stood in grounds on an open boulevard. It was full of fine furniture, the paintings included a large Gainsborough, and it had a well-stocked library. On my first morning I was awakened by an elderly English butler, who, as he drew the curtains, enquired: "What time would you like the car sir,". "I haven't got a car", I replied. "The car that Mr. Leonard has provided for you", was his dignified rejoinder. It seemed too much, so I didn't order it. Downstairs at breakfast Leonard said to me: "I hear you won't use the car". I told him that he was too generous. He replied "I have a Cadillac and chauffeur for the use of my guests, you are the first guest I have had in the last three months; if you won't use the car the chauffeur will probably commit suicide". So, for the rest of my visit, I was rolling around Cleveland in a chauffeur-driven Cadillac.

It was four days before the wedding and each evening there was a party, the first given by Peggy's Bohemian brother Winsor. My capacity for liquor is poor, but I didn't want to let Herbert down; so, before leaving for the party, I had a word with the butler. He appreciated my concern and suggested gravely that before leaving I should take a little olive oil to line my stomach. "What a good idea", I said, "but where shall I get it?" "Just a moment", he said, and, leaving me, soon re-appeared with a silver dessert spoon on a silver salver with a bottle of olive oil from which he gravely dispensed two dessert spoonfuls, which I swallowed under his expert eye. It was a splendid party. The set-piece was a mound of caviare resting in a hollowed pillar of ice in which fronds of ivy were frozen. Vodka and every sort of liquor flowed. Winsor was a good host and he made sure that all his guests were well supplied. It was gay from the start, and still gayer as the party progressed, except for me. The butler's recipe was only too successful. For once in my life my capacity to take in alcohol was unlimited; it was passing through my stomach lined with olive oil without getting into my blood stream. On the way home the roads were a sheet of ice, cars were skidding, and the car I was in did a double spin. What terrific fun for everyone, everyone except me — the only sober one in the party. I have never taken precautions before going to a party since.

As party succeeded party, it seemed to me that the influence of English Edwardian society lingered on in Cleveland. The standard of living was extremely high, the hospitality lavish, and all about one was a feeling of privilege and exclusiveness. In one very large house the hostess, dressed in Edwardian style, conducted an evening *soirée* in her salon. A signed photograph of Edward, Duke of Windsor, prominently displayed, seemed to be the focal point of the proceedings.

I was taken to a small exclusive city luncheon club, and, after the wedding, to a beautiful colonial style farm-house. The owner kept a pack of foxhounds and the huntsman

The Pavilion Hotel

Mother and Father, with my brothers, Charles and Frank, and myself

(Top) Ernest Bevin, Tom Loughton and friend
(Left) Chef Moore, Pavilion Hotel
(Right) Charles Laughton, painted by Ruszkowski

came from Cleveland, Yorkshire. The wealthy Clevelanders had adopted the manners and customs of Edwardian English society.

The wedding took place in the Heaton residence. The chief organiser was an Uncle George, who had a keen eye for detail and was assisted by Peggy's brother Winsor, who amongst other things had produced the band. The wedding had a familiar look to me, which puzzled me until I realised that I had seen similar weddings reproduced in Hollywood films. There was a minor crisis just before the bride appeared at the top of the staircase. Uncle George suddenly decided that the two little kneeling stools covered with white satin would not do, as they looked to him like a pair of babies' funeral caskets, and he insisted that they should be replaced. Later, after the ceremony, Uncle George discovered that he had lost his watch. Winsor, who was responsible for the band, took the loss to himself. "Uncle George has lost his watch", he wailed, "I know my band boys will get the blame". They certainly looked the likeliest culprits — they would have been more at home in a downtown night club than in the Heaton residence.

At the wedding breakfast someone proposed the toast of the British Royal family and everyone rose to their feet to honour it. I was the only Britisher there, apart from the bridegroom, so I decided it would be polite to propose the toast of the American President, Mr. Roosevelt. It was not a success. He was so unpopular with the assembled company that only about a third stood up to drink his health.

After the wedding and before returning home, I wanted to see as much as possible of American hotels. In Cleveland I was introduced by the manager of one of the large hotels to the organising secretary of a conference of Men's Wear specialists. In response to my interest, he invited me to attend the remaining two days of the conference. I accepted, said goodbye to my host Leonard Hannah, and took up residence in the conference hotel, a label pinned to my lapel. I attended the business sessions, enjoyed the hospitality of clothing manufacturers, and was placed at the top table for the final banquet. When I asked for my bill I was told that I had been a guest of the association. The secretary was most informative. The conference was held annually and to get the accommodation they required, the bookings were made two years ahead. He pointed out that his association was only one of hundreds of others that held conferences every year.

From Cleveland I moved on to the school of hotel-keeping at Cornell University, where I was invited to give a talk. The lecture hall was surrounded by heavy apparatus, compressors, refrigerators, air-conditioners and the like; engineering seemed to get more attention than the creation of comfortable surroundings and good food. I chose as my subject "The Chef Proprietors of France", feeling that I was striking a blow for individualism. After my talk the company adjourned to the hostelry to drink and to sing. I was pressed to make a solo contribution; eventually with trepidation I attempted to sing unaccompanied "On Ilkla Moor Baht 'at". I was not sure that I knew all the words, but they came to me as the song progressed.

From Cornell I returned to New York, where I was the guest of Lucius Boomer, the president and active controller of the Waldorf Astoria. He gave me the use of a Tower Apartment and invited me to go where I liked throughout the whole of his enormous hotel. It would have taken months to absorb all there was to be seen.

The Tower Apartment looked over a wonderful panorama of the city. At night the view was breathtaking but astonishingly lonely. Surrounded by millions of people and millions of lights and yet I was alone — not a very happy situation. Still there was plenty to occupy me. One of the specialities at the Waldorf Astoria was catering for Jewish weddings, the surroundings for which could be astonishing. No novelty seemed too bizarre to proclaim the wealth of the participants. Flowers were twisted into the most astounding shapes, as though something novel had to be created regardless of cost. It was the same in the penthouse restaurant and the ballroom, where many of the most fashionable New York functions took place. The cost of the setting alone for some of the parties I saw must have run into thousands of dollars.

Most interesting of all to me was Mr. Boomer's sales promotion department, with files stacked with particulars of all the organisations that ran conferences and of all the social functions. The daily papers were searched to spot any new potential in the market. Throughout my stay there was a constant succession of conferences, sometimes three or four taking place on the same day, and every day letters and telegrams were poured out from the sales promotion office to conferences taking place in other parts of the country, suggesting that the Waldorf be chosen for their next meeting.

The hotel was fascinating and so was the city. The art galleries – the Metropolitan, the Museum of Modern Art, the Frick – were stacked with masterpieces. The one I remember best was "The Harvest", one of the great masterpieces of the world, by Pieter Brueghel. At the Frick it was heartbreaking to see Holbein's portrait of Sir Thomas More; how could it have been allowed to leave England? The galleries were well run; much better run than ours. The details were so good: good lifts, good cloakrooms, well run cafeterias, good bookstalls and a plethora of well informed staff.

The Christmas season was approaching and New York was transformed. Scintillating Christmas trees were erected on every available ledge, and Christmas carols rang out from loud speakers on every side. The store windows were

decked with gorgeous Christmas presents; love, love, love
— give, give, give — buy, buy, buy — was the inescapable
message. The Waldorf Astoria was not to be outdone. On
Christmas Eve a choir of real choir boys in red cassocks
and white surplices sang in the imposing entrance hall.

Christmas alone at the Waldorf was too much for me.
On Christmas Eve I attended midnight Mass at St. Patrick's, the Roman Catholic cathedral situated near the
hotel. When I arrived at the cathedral it was already
packed, but I managed to find a place to stand not far
from the cathedral doors. Latecomers kept arriving, some
of them forcing their way brutally through the standing
congregation, with elbows raised regardless of all else save
themselves. I was standing near a pillar when an elbow was
thrust into the face of a woman standing beside me; I
managed to protect her with my arm. The atmosphere was
ruined for me, I turned to leave and the woman I had pro-
tected came with me. We adjourned to a nearby bar; instead of taking communion in the cathedral we drank
together in the bar and she invited me to her apartment.
When I arrived back at the Waldorf I, too, had celebrated
Christmas Eve.

Back in my Tower Apartment I looked over the Man-
hattan landscape feeling disgusted with myself and more
alone than ever. Christmas dinner alone in one of the
Waldorf restaurants was the last straw. Suddenly I had an
overwhelming feeling that I must get home. There was a
German liner sailing for Europe two days after Christmas.
I booked a berth and said goodbye to Mr. Boomer, thank-
ing him for his generous hospitality. The ship was almost
empty, the food was poor, but I did not care; for every
day on board was bringing me nearer home.

CHAPTER XII

FIRST STEPS IN BURGUNDY

On the way home, I stayed for a few nights in London with Charles and Elsa in their new home in Gordon Square. He had come back to England to work with Korda after his enormous success playing Captain Bligh in *Mutiny on the Bounty*. He got on well with Korda, who directed him in the film *Rembrandt* in which Charles gave one of his best performances. Korda's next film was *I Claudius*, based on the book by Robert Graves; this time, he gave the direction to Josef Von Sternberg. Charles found Sternberg unsympathetic and uncongenial. Before I left for America I had had a brief glimpse of Sternberg on the set at Denham Studios. Clad in riding breeches and tasselled Hessian boots, his head swathed in a turban and carrying in his hand a riding switch, he looked more like a circus ring-master than a film director.

Charles was intensely interested in the *I Claudius* part and was basing his performance on a close study of the book and its sources, rather than on the script, which he thought inept. He told me that Sternberg seemed to have no conception of what he was trying to do. It was a difficult situation, finally resolved by the sudden collapse of the production. The reason given was the illness of Merle Oberon, the female lead, who became incapacitated owing to a mysterious taxi accident. The expenses of the production were recouped from the City and the artists with broken contracts were compensated. Charles' share of the pay-out was forty thousand pounds. He was disappointed, as he had become obsessed by the part. but he was not sorry to see the last of Sternberg.

It was the *I Claudius* episode that caused Charles to part company with Korda and to embark on setting up a film company of his own in which he hoped to have greater artistic freedom. The company was "Mayflower Films" which he set up in association with John Maxwell, a Scottish lawyer and film financier, and Erich Pommer, a continental film director.

When I arrived at Gordon Square, I found Charles full of the new project, with Elsa looking on with a sceptical eye. She was concentrating on running their new home. She had the luck to engage Nellie Boxall as their cook. Nellie had come over from the house of Virginia Woolf, who lived across the square. Virginia had suddenly conceived the idea that Nellie had been with her too long, so Nellie had moved over. Now she was blossoming under the rapturous appreciation of Charles and the practical collaboration of Elsa. The results were impressive.

In all the excitement of the new film company there was little room for the plans that were seething in my brain. Charles was so much on the crest of the wave that he was inclined to scout any ideas other than his own. Hotel considerations were a mere distraction, so after a few days I left for home, dazzled and even maybe a little depressed by such success; a success I could never hope to match.

Back at home, I was soon immersed in the practical problems of the hotel; preparing for re-opening at Easter, and, more important, working on the plans for the transformation of the hotel.

I spent hours with Harry Johnson, describing the American conferences, giving him my view that conferences would be the hotel business of the future — explaining the need for meeting-rooms, banqueting accommodation and the need for flexibility. I was in time. Harry had prepared his *avant projet* drawings for his treatment of the exterior, but he was not yet at the detailed planning stage. Now we were able to plan a dual purpose hotel, catering in the summer for the holiday makers and, during the rest of the year, for conferences of every kind.

It was not an easy task, as by now we had come to appreciate the quality of the architecture of the hotel. Designed by one of the Wyatt brothers in the early nineteenth century, the interior architecture had a rare distinction. It had been pillaged and neglected over the years, but the basic quality of the architectural design remained. There was a great deal to be done to bring back the original distinction, and in the meantime nothing had to be done that would not blend with and add to the quality that was already there.

Harry proved himself to be a sensitive and intelligent architect who understood the policy I was trying to create, and, at the same time, appreciated the quality of the existing hotel. His plans had to provide for more than doubling the capacity of the restaurant, lounges and bar, which he managed to do without unduly interfering with the best architectural features. At this stage the plans were only on paper, and we were now faced with the additional problem of catering for the conference business. Services had to be enlarged, furniture stores provided, and the new accommodation re-planned to accommodate meetings and banquets. My music room, littered with plans, became like an architect's office and it was a considerable time before we were satisfied.

The next thing was the finance. I claimed that the additional conference business would more than double the turnover and treble the net profit. I made my second trip to the city, again to Barclay's head office. I returned with the finance arranged, so that the contracts could be let and the work carried out the following winter.

Chef Tognoli returned from Italy to take charge of the kitchens. This year the small brigade of chefs was stronger. I had managed to engage two additional chefs to strengthen the top end of his team, an elderly French sauce cook with first class experience, and a good larder chef. I persuaded Tognoli to limit the range of menus, so that what was produced would be of first class quality; the result was encouraging.

In the spring an elderly French woman, the dowager Comtesse de Lavoreille, stayed with us for a fortnight and she was most appreciative. She had noticed the quality of the consommé and the quality of the sauces; she said that they were the best she had come across in England. Before she left she told me that her family owned vineyards on the Côte de Beaune and the Côte de Nuits, and she promised to send me a case of their wine. The case arrived in the early summer, but I didn't taste it until later in the year.

When I drank it, it was a revelation. I had drunk fine Bordeaux wines, but never before had I tasted good quality Burgundy, as at that time it was a rarity in England. The English shippers of Burgundy seemed to have the theory that English Burgundy drinkers had a taste for heavy wine. The Burgundy I had been used to drinking had been blended — blended by the shippers to satisfy the mythical English taste, which I think they had created so that the taste could be satisfied at more profit to themselves. The wines sent to me by the Comtesse were delicious, each with a delicate aroma, individual character, and delightful to drink. I had never enjoyed wine so much. I wrote to thank her, and at the same time to enquire whether it would be possible to purchase wine of similar quality for the hotel cellars. The outcome of our correspondence was an invitation to stay with her eldest son, the Comte de Lavoreille, and his family at their Château in Santenay. I accepted for a visit at the end of the season, after the hotel had closed down.

It was a busy summer for me, running the hotel with unfamiliar staff, building up a style of catering to match the resources at my disposal, and, at the front of the house, organising a social programme to liven up and compensate for the drab condition of the hotel. On top of this, I was finalising the plans for the re-organisation, arranging the finance, applying for planning permission, and eventually going out to tender. It was all done in time — contracts were let so that the builders were able to take over immediately after the hotel closed down at the end of the season. Soon after the builders came in, I left for my trip to Burgundy.

I travelled by train to Dijon, taking a car from there to Santenay. Passing along the Côte de Nuits, I saw the Burgundy vineyards for the first time. The road between Dijon and Beaune runs along the foot of the slopes on which are produced some of the world's most famous wines. We passed Gevrey Chambertin and Clos Vougeot with its magnificent château standing above the enclosed vineyard, into and through the small town of Nuits St. Georges, and from there onto the slopes of the Côte de Beaune. Beaune itself, a beautiful historic town, is the commercial centre of the Burgundy world. After Beaune we passed Pommard, Volnay, Meursault and Montrachet and then branched off the main road to Santenay.

Santenay was little more than a village. The Château, with a raised stone terrace was the principal building facing on to the square, but set back on the wide terrace, it enjoyed complete privacy. My host and hostess, the Comte and Comtesse de Lavoreille, met me on the terrace with their children round them — three beautiful girls and a young boy. None of them spoke a word of English and my poor French accent and my still poorer vocabulary convulsed the children. I was taken to my room. Everything in the Château seemed faded and even a little spartan, but the over-all effect for me was of another country and another time — eighteenth century France. There were one or two concessions to more recent times, a haphazard system of fragile electric wiring and some remarkable plumbing. The water closet was tucked away in a remote little room off the terrace; it was equipped with a beautifully decorated pedestal closet with a large hinged can, precariously poised above. The children took me in hand and very soon they managed to enlarge my vocabulary, not without a good deal of giggling and outright laughter; they seemed to accept me as a heaven-sent source of light relief.

My more serious education began at dinner. It was my first experience of food in a French home, prepared and served in the French style, and accompanied by the delicious white and red wines of the Lavoreille family vineyards. After dinner we sat by the wood fire in the salon, taking coffee with Marc de Bourgogne. Marc is the spirit distilled from the skins, pips and stalks of the grapes left after the juice is extracted, which if well made and kept long enough can be delicious. The children participated by sucking large lumps of sugar dipped into their parents' glasses and by taking a full part in the conversation of their elders. I had little to say, overwhelmed, as I was, by the novelty and pleasure of the occasion.

The following morning I was taken down steps leading from the château courtyard into the cellars where I was conducted round by Monsieur Rocher, the manager of the estate, who lived with his family in a house across the courtyard. In the vaulted cellars were rows of wine barrels, their contents in various stages of production, some of them still fermenting. In the cellar, I observed the cellarman going round the fermenting barrels, gently filling them through the vent with minute quantities of wine from an ancient can not unlike a battered old watering can with a candle sconce close to the end of the spout. I was invited to try some of the previous year's wine, the cellarman dipping a glass pipette into the barrel, then closing the pipette top with his thumb, withdrawing the pipette, and carefully releasing the wine into a little silver tastevin cup, for me to inspect and taste. It was a ceremony with which I was soon familiar. A day or two later I was to buy my own tastevin — a beautiful shallow silver cup which is still one of my prized possessions.

My hosts took my education seriously. I was taken to many vineyards, and at each no trouble seemed to be too much when showing me the range and quality of their wines. Wherever I went I met the same dedication — the overwhelming interest in the production of good wine. I was privileged to be meeting the wine growers, not the wine dealers — there is a wide gap between the two.

Towards the end of my visit I was taken to the Domaine de la Romanée Conti to taste the wines of this world famous property. An old man in carpet slippers came out of the residence and conducted us into the cellars. After a little polite conversation he proceeded to let me taste some of his 1933 vintage wines; Romanée Conti, La Tâche and Richebourg are the ones that I remember. I had been tasting many fine wines but none quite as good as these. After I had tasted several wines, the old man asked me to express my opinion. I told him that I preferred the La Tâche first and the Richebourg Domaine de la Romanée Conti second. He seemed surprised, and turning to my host he said, "Mais j'ai pensé qu'il était un Anglais!" "Oui", the count replied. "Incroyable", said the old man. I asked if it was possible to buy some of his wine, "Certainly", he said, "What would you like?". In my ignorance I asked for a hogshead of each, that is twenty-four dozen of La Tâche Domaine de la Romanée Conti 1933 and twenty-four dozen Richebourg Domaine de la Romanée Conti 1933. There was a stunned silence. I could tell by my host's face that I had made a most unwarranted request, but not in the eyes of the old proprietor. "Certainly", he said, and in the course of time the wine arrived in the cellars of the Royal Hotel at Scarborough. Many years later I served a bottle of the La Tâche to Pat Guimaraens when he was staying with me at home. Later, during the meal, he spoke of its quality and remarked "You are not selling this wine are you, Tom?" "Yes", I replied, "it is on the hotel list". "Well", he said, "you are an idiot".

The La Tâche and the Richebourg headed the substantial list of my purchases. It is difficult to understand how I had the nerve to plunge so deeply. Amongst the red wines I purchased were Santenay, Les Gravières; Volnay, Les Caillerets, Clos de la Pousse d'Or; Pommard, Les Rugiens and Les Epenots; Nuits St. Georges, Les St. Georges, Les Porrets and Les Pruliers; Chambolle Musigny, Les Bonnes Mares; Gevrey Chambertin, Clos St. Jacques and Chambertin. The white wines included: Puligny Montrachet, Le Montrachet, Meursault, Les Santenots blancs, Aloxe Corton, and Corton Charlemagne, every one of them purchased in the cellars of the Domaine from impeccable growers. All were known by my host to be utterly reliable, and every vintage chosen had either his approval or the approval of Mademoiselle Rocher who on occasions was my guide.

At one step I had founded the best cellar of Burgundy in the north of England, with not a single bottle of blended wine in it — all due to the kindness of the dowager Comtesse de Lavoreille.

I stayed over three weeks and came away a fervent Burgundy fan. I returned each succeeding year until the war broke out, and during the pre-war years filled the Burgundy section of our cellars to bursting point. In 1938 I was invited to attend the banquet of the Confrérie des Chevaliers de Tastevin in the cellars of the Clos de Vougeot and I was made a Commandeur of the Confrérie. The Confrérie is a kind of public relations operation conducted with enthusiasm and imagination, assisted by the benign influence of the product it is there to publicise. I came away from the banquet well primed, and with a feeling that I had been canonised.

On my first visit, I stopped off at the Hôtel de la Côte d'Or at Saulieu for a few nights on the recommendation of Charles. The proprietor, Alexandre Dumaine, was an old friend of Charles and was one of the leading chefs of France. I was received by Madame Dumaine, a charming, spare, reserved woman. Monsieur Dumaine was formidable, large and ebullient — no wonder — for if ever there was a master of his craft it was Monsieur Dumaine. Never before had I experienced such cooking. There must have been some Burgundian bush telegraph as he knew of my wine purchases, and he made it his business to further my experience from the very extensive resources of his cellar.

I have often had perfection at home in the form of simple dishes perfectly cooked. This is the sort of food that I prefer. At the Hôtel de la Côte d'Or the food was not simple, but for once in my experience, Monsieur Dumaine's elaborate preparation and cooking was justified by the marvellous dishes he produced. He loved his craft and he lived to practise it. One year we attended the banquet at Clos Vougeot together. The Burgundians treated him like a prince, recognising him as a prince amongst chefs.

I arrived at his hotel on one occasion to find Madame Dumaine distressed. I enquired what was the trouble. "Oh", she said, "my husband, what an impossible man; what do you think? We were expecting some important Parisians for lunch and they arrived two hours late. Alexandre received them himself, took them into the kitchen and pointed to their lunch spoiling on the stove. He turned to the saucier and said, 'Henri, open the stove top'. He then threw the dish on to the fire! 'Now', he said to his guests; 'if you care to wait, I will cook you another lunch, if not, good afternoon' ". I told Madame Dumaine that she was a lucky woman to have a husband who could afford to be so independent.

On the way back I stayed with Charles and Elsa for a few days but things were not the same. Charles was obsessed with the affairs of the new film company, and he seemed to be living in a state of constant crisis. He was deeply embroiled with his new associates, Erich Pommer and John Maxwell. Up till that time he had had only one thing to worry about – his own acting; now his worries seemed to be legion, and they were reflected in the life at Gordon Square. To me, an outsider, the film business appeared to be a cloud cuckoo land where there are no ducks, only swans, and where the weather alternates between blissful sunshine and raging tempests.

There had been a minor tempest the night before my arrival, which had blown John Armstrong into oblivion. He had left the house in an alcoholic rage and had vanished. Benita, his girl friend, Elsa and Charles, had no idea as to what had happened to him, and they could talk of little else. After supper, on the evening of my arrival, the telephone rang. Elsa picked it up, it was John. "Where are you?" queried Elsa, "Glasgow, ducky", was his reply, "and I haven't any money". He had rushed out of the house to the nearest railway station – Euston – and he had taken the first available train – which happened to be for Glasgow. To my relief he was back the next day. It was important for me as he was doing the décor for the ground floor of the Royal.

John showed me the preliminary sketches in his Charlotte Street studio; they had the theatrical touch for which I was hoping – especially his designs for the ballroom on a Neptune theme. He suggested that colour stage lighting should be used and he had the idea of a theatrical projector lantern to be built into the ceiling. This would project moving cloud effects on the wall behind a lighthouse to be erected on the canopy above the band dais. We went together to the theatrical lighting specialists and arranged for a complete stage lighting switchboard and for a cloud effect lantern.

I met Erich Pommer the producer. He reminded me of Alexander Korda — a man full of ideas, but ideas that were liable to be very expensive to those associated with him. I had a feeling that the collaboration of Pommer with Charles was very much a fair-weather association. There seemed to be a euphoria about the whole project which had enveloped Charles but not Elsa; she was looking on with a sceptical eye.

I left for home feeling worried about Charles. He was getting immersed in business which seemed to me alien to his true vocation. I knew it would be no good saying anything, as his enormous success had made him very difficult to criticise. In any case I had plenty of worries of my own, and it was time that I was back at home to deal with them.

CHAPTER XIII

BRIEF INTERLUDE AT ELSTREE

Harry Johnson was waiting for me at the hotel with plenty of problems. The need for large banqueting rooms involved the use of heavy steel beams, and he was finding the size of steel girders which he required difficult to obtain. The conversion of one of the bedroom wings to give more accommodation had proved to be too heavy for the existing structure, so that steel girders had to be inserted between the floors. Such things were to be expected in a hundred year old building. Harry was worried about the time of completion and about the additional cost. I was able to reassure him as I had friends in the steel business and I was able to get the deliveries he was asking for. If only the alterations were successful in creating the hotel for which I was looking, the additional cost would be a secondary consideration.

His plans to join together the restaurant and lounges into one large banqueting hall involved two sets of folding glass door. These, if left plain, were going to look stark and uninviting. This was solved by John Armstrong designing a history of sail in the form of a series of drawings of ships from primitive sailing vessels to modern racing yachts, and these designs were cut into the glass panels. I thought they might be vulnerable to breakages, but they have survived intact for over thirty years. For the ballroom John had designed beautiful linen curtains in cerulean blue, on which were printed a line of coloured flags that ran from floor to ceiling. Theatrical lighting battens were concealed in bulkheads which ran the length of the room, the colour of the lighting being controlled from the theatrical lighting board built in a small control room behind the bandstand. The ballroom was going to be one of the outstanding features of the hotel.

The main decoration in the new bar was to be a large drawing of sailors and girls cut into a blue gesso panel rather in the nature of a large, decorative, blue print. The main effect came from a massive brass counter and brass-topped tables made by an old fashioned firm of brass founders in Hull. The drawing was to be cut into the panel by John shortly before the opening. There was to be considerable work for John to do at the last minute, but I knew he would manage so long as we could keep him going with supplies of Guinness.

The re-opening was fixed for mid-May, so that the hotel bookings could be accepted from June onwards. One of the problems was how to publicise the new image of the hotel. I eventually decided that an effective method would be to stage a lavish re-opening party on a date when Charles could attend, as any re-appearance of Charles in Scarborough automatically attracted wide publicity.

When the date was fixed, Charles, who by now was becoming interested, suggested that we should employ Constance Spry to do the flower decorations for the party. Constance was a friend of Charles, and she agreed to send one of her best girls up from London. She came a few days beforehand to enable her to assess the floral resources of the district. This she did, and she produced a magnificent show without having to send for many flowers from London.

The night before the party Charles and Elsa arrived, and we had dinner together with John Armstrong, Benita, Eric Fenby and Bruce Turner. The conversation turned to Delius. Charles was especially interested in his incidental music for Flecker's Hassan. Charles could quote some of the long speeches, and to the surprise of Charles, Eric could follow him on the piano with a condensation of the lovely musical themes.

After dinner we inspected the hotel. Charles was struck by John's Neptune ballroom, and by the system of theatrical lighting. Eric mounted the band dais and began to play incidental music as the changing colours played on the walls of the ballroom. Charles joined him on the dais and began to speak passages from Hassan, Eric playing the Delius music. I have never heard Charles' beautiful voice used to better effect. At that moment I had the conviction that the hotel was different, and that it was going to be a success.

Five to six hundred guests came to the opening party. The presence of Charles and Elsa was important, but it was the transformation of the hotel that was the real sensation. Entertainment was provided by two dance bands — one playing in the new lounge, in which there was a sprung maple floor — the other in the ballroom with the stage lighting being used to its full effect. A buffet, theatrical in its lavishness, ran the full length of the enlarged dining room. Champagne was served throughout the evening with a choice of a white and red burgundy, both of unusual quality.

The thing that impressed the guests most was the new bar, which was going at full stretch ladling out every form of bar drink, with no charge from the beginning until the end of the evening. As far as I know there were no casualties apart from one or two battered traffic bollards in the car parks close by the hotel.

The party was reported in the press and the bush telegraph buzzed. In a short space of time it was known throughout a very wide area that the Royal had re-opened and that the hotel was transformed. The party gave sufficient publicity — business poured in and although the capacity of the hotel was considerably increased it was filled throughout the season.

Not long after the party, I had a telephone call from

Charles. He was unhappy and wanted me to go up to London to have a talk with him. I went up as soon as I could, to find Charles worried and depressed, he was finding his additional business responsibilities too much to cope with. He was beginning to realise that the financial demands of the film company were getting him into deep water as more and more finance was required and Charles was getting to the end of his resources. John Maxwell was in the background ready to fill the gap but his price was Charles having to sign a long-term contract with him, a price Charles was not willing to pay. He was regretting the death of Irving Thalberg of Metro Goldwyn Mayer; the association with him had produced such films as *The Barretts of Wimpole Street* and *Mutiny on the Bounty*; it was inconceivable to him to consider replacing Irving Thalberg by John Maxwell. The difficulty lay in his present close association with Maxwell, since he could not bring himself to tell him openly that he would not extend it. Charles had the extraordinary idea that I was the man to extricate him from his difficulties, even though I knew nothing about the film business. "I want you to run my business affairs", he said, "and I want you to deal with Maxwell". It seemed an impossible task for me to take on, but I promised that at the end of our summer season I would do what I could to help him.

It was a long season lasting well into October and it was in October that the hotel had its most important guest, Winston Churchill. When Churchill arrived I took him to his suite, and before leaving him I asked whether he would prefer to dine in the suite or in the restaurant. He looked slowly around; it was a delightful room with a view across the harbour, the Castle Hill in the background and a statue of Queen Victoria in the foreground. The surroundings seemed to give him satisfaction. "I will dine here", he said, so I told him that a waiter would be sent to take his order. "No", he said, "I will leave it to you". Fortunately we had some knowledge of his tastes, as Chef Schaerer, who succeeded Chef Tognoli, had been soup chef at the Ritz Hotel, London, during the First World War when it was frequented by Churchill. Through the Chef we knew that he liked consommé, Dover soles, underdone Scotch beef, saddles of lamb and the like, so it was clear that if we confined ourselves to simple dishes made from the best English produce he would be suited.

I had laid in a supply of Pol Roger champagne, and had a particularly good Fine Champagne Cognac, so that his tastes in that direction were catered for. He stayed for five days and during his stay he did not order a single dish. After his first meal he coined a phrase to deal with his requirements — "I leave it entirely to you", and all the time we managed to satisfy him. On the last evening he gave a dinner party, preliminary to his appearing on the platform for the Prime Minister's speech to the Conservative Conference. At the meeting I was told that Churchill settled himself down in his seat on the platform, fell asleep and snored his way through Neville Chamberlain's oration.

After the meal one of the waiters who had served the dinner came to me and reported a piece of Churchill's conversation. Among his guests was a local landowner, the Earl of Feversham. The waiter had heard Churchill say, "I say Feversham, I bet you didn't know there was a damned good hotel like this in your district; it takes a fellow like me to find out these things".

At the end of the season, as soon as the hotel closed down for the winter, I rushed off to Burgundy, staying first with Monsieur Dumaine at Saulieu and from there went on to Chablis to stay with Monsieur Bergerand at his old fashioned but comfortable Hôtel de l'Etoile. I had an introduction to Monsieur Bergerand from Monsieur Dumaine, and when I arrived at the hotel I was told that Monsieur Bergerand was out in the vineyards. The best vineyards of Chablis lie across the River Serein close to the little town, so I crossed the bridge and walked towards them. In one of them I saw a white-coated figure leading a horse through the vines; it was Monsieur Bergerand, still in his chef's clothes, working in the vineyard.

Staying with Monsieur Bergerand I was able to taste the Grands Crus of Chablis in company with some of his notable dishes. It was the season for game, and we had woodcock, partridge and wild boar. One dish I remember — a capon generously larded with truffles dug up in the local woodland. During the day I wandered through the vineyards, calling haphazardly at little farms where I was always made welcome and invited to taste the wines in their cellars. I learnt to appreciate the distinctive flinty taste and the exquisite golden green colour of true Chablis.

From Chablis I went back to Saulieu for a night with Monsieur and Madame Dumaine. The start of my dinner on the first evening was a delicious cream of pheasant. I asked Monsieur Dumaine how long it had taken to prepare, "Three days", was his reply. From Saulieu I went on to Santenay, but this time I was staying with Monsieur and Madame Rocher as the Lavoreille family were in Paris. Madame Rocher was a splendid cook who took her seat at the table after the main course was served. I had found the food in the Château good, but it was not as good as the food cooked by Madame Rocher.

During this visit I was conducted round the vineyards by Mademoiselle Rocher. She had a comprehensive knowledge of the Burgundy world and she knew where the outstanding wines of the previous year were to be found. We visited the Château de Meursault, and in the cellars the proprietor, the Comte de Moucheron, showed me a 1929 Gevrey Chambertin Clos St. Jacques with a bouquet that was reminiscent of scented violets. I was able to purchase ten dozen bottles of this wine, and I also took a single case to take back with me for Charles at Gordon Square. This time my stay in Santenay was short, as I felt it imperative to get back to Charles.

Back in Gordon Square, I found Charles desperately worried. He was discovering what a nightmare the business of film production can be, especially for a company with limited resources. The company was in the process of making its third film. In each one the costs had come out far above the original estimate; part of this was due to Charles, as his search for perfection in his own performances was costing a fantastic amount of money. He had taken a part in the financing of the Mayflower Picture Corporation, to give himself scope to film in this country. Now he was finding that the company he had helped to finance was turning into an octopus which was squeezing the life out of him. His money was running out; the power was now in the hands of John Maxwell, who was in a position to provide the additional finance or to let the company go bankrupt. Charles wanted me to negotiate with Maxwell on his behalf, and to give me the necessary authority he handed over to me all his business affairs and gave me his power of attorney. I never knew what Elsa thought about it, but I did know she was not enthusiastic about the Mayflower company. I think she must have thought that things were so bad that I could not make them much worse.

I found myself attending meeting after meeting, going to interminable lunches at the Ecu de France and the Etoile — the time for business seemed to be over the coffee and cigars. To bring myself into the picture I started to smoke Havana cigars, and as I had never smoked before, my smoking technique must have emphasised my amateur status.

With all the talk the one paramount factor was the finance. The company was in the hands of Maxwell and nothing would save it if he refused to provide further money. I had to deal with him at his home in Portland Place — usually late in the evening over a whisky and soda.

He kept telling me how fond he was of Charles and how much he admired his acting ability, but if he had to risk more capital in the present venture he must have the security of a long term contract for his services. He knew that Charles' financial resources were exhausted and thought he had him. Eventually I had to tell him that whatever happened Charles would not sign a long contract with him. He took it badly. All I could do was to tell him that Charles would fulfil his obligations as an actor, and that he would be at the studio as long as the production team was functioning. Mr. Maxwell accused me of trying to blackmail him, so I left.

The next day I got a message that Maxwell had decided to provide the money without conditions, and that he was off to the South of France for three weeks' holiday. When he came back from the South of France the money ran out again, but he did not make any further trouble; he provided the finance required to finish the film without attempting to impose any additional conditions.

The film was *Jamaica Inn,* based on the novel by Daphne du Maurier, and adapted by Clemence Dane, a friend of Charles. Charles was playing the villain. In the novel the villain was the village parson, but as one of the conventions of the screen was that a clergyman must not be represented as a villain another character had to be found for the purpose — the character chosen was the village squire. The trouble with the film production was that Charles couldn't play the part as written. The director of the film was Alfred Hitchcock, who was a close friend of Charles. There was a good cast including a beautiful young newcomer to films, Maureen O'Hara.

All the sets were built, and filming was proceeding with everything and everyone except Charles. There was nothing for it but to have the part for Charles rewritten. J.B. Priestley was brought in, to write his version of the character, and that is how it was eventually played. The situation was that ninety thousand pounds had been spent, and there was not a single shot of Charles that could be used!

I was staying with Charles in Gordon Square, and Elsa was away in America. Charles arrived back from the Elstree studios at supper time in a state of desperation. "Let's get drunk, Charles", I said and went for a bottle of Clos St. Jacques. We drank Clos St. Jacques before our meal, during the meal and after. I don't know how many bottles we consumed but I do know we drank too many — it was delicious. After the meal we were sitting on the couch facing the magnificent Renoir with the three glorious nudes. The wine had an extraordinary effect on Charles, he kept leaping up, striding round the room, and using the most frightful language about Pommer, Hitchcock and Maxwell. I sat on the couch meekly endorsing his curses; all I could say was, "Yes, Charles, yes, Charles". Had I said anything else there is no doubt he would have turned on me. At length we crawled up to bed, Charles had only one flight to go, I had two but I made it.

The next morning Charles had to be up very early; his make-up included a false top to his head and a large wax nose so that it was a very long process. I got up much later, none the worse for the previous night's excesses. Nellie Boxall cooked and served my breakfast. "How was Charles?" I asked. Nellie gave me a pained look. "Didn't you hear him in the bathroom during the night?" she asked. "No, Nellie", I said, "Oh dear", said Nellie, "he was so ill I thought he'd bring his heart up, and this morning he could scarcely speak". My own heart sank; my desperate remedy had made him ill. I made my way out to Elstree, where I had a privileged position — I was treated as though I was one of the financiers and for the first time in my life I was finding people opening doors for me. As the studio door-keeper opened the door he whispered into my ear, "He's got it, he's playing the part". In the studio there on the set, was an eighteenth century squire drinking port and cracking nuts — he was away with it! The film was finished in a very short period, and I believe in the end it didn't lose money, it may even have made a little. Charles and I had saved ninety thousand pounds by drinking burgundy. It was a pity that the bulk of the money belonged to John Maxwell.

Hollywood was missing Charles, and approaches from the major American film companies kept coming to him. One of his difficulties was his involved position with the Mayflower company. A director of the American film company R.K.O. came over from Hollywood prepared to take over all Charles' Mayflower obligations, and to make a contract to pay him one hundred and fifty thousand pounds for five films. The thing that attracted Charles was the take over of his Mayflower liabilities, so the contract was completed.

A surprising factor was that R.K.O. wanted to sign me up as well. I never enquired in what capacity. I had seen enough of the film world, if an actor with the capability of Charles had such a struggle to maintain his freedom, what chance would I have had? In any case I had plenty of my own liabilities at home and I intended to face them.

So Charles returned to America, this time to settle down and eventually to become a naturalised American citizen, and I returned to hotel-keeping in Scarborough.

CHAPTER XIV

THE NUNS TAKE OVER

It was a relief to be back at the hotel, free from the distractions and stresses of the film world. I had envied Charles in the early days of his theatrical successes, but I no longer did. I was content to be back in a world in which I had a more secure footing and where I felt at home. There was a stability and a discipline about my life in the hotel that was very different from the volatile atmosphere of the film world.

The discipline needed at the Royal was especially rigid, as the seasonal conditions made it extremely difficult to establish the standard of catering that I was struggling to attain. The first step had been to re-organise and re-equip the kitchens. The main kitchen had a new central stove, stock-pot and consommé stands, tilting soup kettles, a comprehensive battery of substantial copper pans and stainless steel tables throughout. The kitchens now had an hygienic and efficient appearance. It was difficult to realise that the kitchen was actually well over one hundred years old, as was evidenced by the roasting spit gear which I had left on the wall perched above the consommé and stock-pot stands.

The difficulty lay in establishing each season the sound classical methods of kitchen practice, when each season there was a new brigade of chefs. When I took over the Royal, Chef Tognoli had given up the struggle, but with my support he had re-established the methods with which he had grown up, and he had needed my constant support to maintain them.

The new chef had first-class experience and I managed

to surround him with well trained departmental chefs. The difficulty lay with the younger men, most of whom had not had a proper training and who found difficulty in accepting the instructions of the older men. Each season I had to build up as good a team of chefs as were available and then make certain that from the start of the season proper methods were established and maintained, and that shoddy and unsound methods did not creep in. Without supervision, chefs are very inclined to prepare and cook food far in advance so that it has to be kept hot, and in many cases has to be warmed up. Timing is a most important factor; in a large kitchen, with a full brigade of chefs serving table d'hôte meals, it is extremely difficult to co-ordinate the chefs' work so that the food comes out of the kitchen into the food services straight from the stove top, or fresh from the ovens. To attain anything approaching a reasonable standard there was no alternative to the maintenance of constant supervision. I accepted it and I enjoyed the appreciation with which the customers responded.

Winston Churchill had not been my only important guest in the 1937 season. Someone else, not so important in the eyes of the world but more important to me, had turned up unexpectedly. I had a telephone call from Madge; she was coming north for York Races, could she have a suite and accommodation for her chauffeur? She arrived looking more glamorous than ever in a chauffeur-driven Lagonda. It was an exciting visit for me, I had not seen her since her marriage, and her attraction was as strong as ever. When she came back from the races we spent our evenings together; on one occasion we were joined by Eric Fenby. After dinner he played for us in my music room. I had never heard him play better — like me he had fallen under her spell.

She returned twice a year for the spring and summer York meetings until the outbreak of war in 1939. Before

I joined the army I went down to see her in her country house in Bedfordshire. She had given birth to a son and she wanted me to see him. It was the last time that we met, although I was to hear from her again.

When war came the hotel quickly emptied. Almost all the holiday guests left, and in their place we had an influx of convent girls evacuated from Hull; the girls were accompanied by nuns including a formidable Reverend Mother. The nuns soon settled in; there was no chaos and imperceptibly the Reverend Mother took charge of the hotel. The sudden transition made me realise that for the time being my hotel-keeping days were over and that I had to find another job. I thought of two things — joining the local regiment, the Green Howards, or joining the Army Catering Corps. The latter seemed to fit my qualifications so I wrote to the War Office asking for an interview at their headquarters. I received a letter by return of post fixing an appointment with Sir Isidore Salmon, the Honorary Catering Adviser to the Army.

Before leaving for the interview I called on the Reverend Mother and asked her to pray for me. It was a good thing I did so, for without her prayers I am sure that I should not have been able to cope with Sir Isidore.

The appointment was for 5 p.m. at the office of the Army Catering Corps commanding officer, Lieutenant-Colonel Byford. The interview with Sir Isidore was an ordeal. He was a small man, a Napoleon of the hotel and catering world, the Chairman of Lyons, the most successful catering company in Great Britain, and an experienced Member of Parliament. He was shrewd, dictatorial, with a hard exterior, but I was to discover that he had a responsive and understanding core.

The interview took the normal course. He extracted my background, learnt what I was doing at the time, and very soon he put his finger on my weakness which was my lack of catering training. "Can you cook?" he asked, "No",

I had to reply. "What, you can't cook?" he said, "you are no good". His brutal candour got me on the raw. "You may think I'm no good", I said, "but I am damned good" and with that I got up to go. As I reached the door he called me back, "Just a moment, I want you to come and see me tomorrow". "No", I replied, "what is the good?" His eyes glistened, "Now, my boy", he said, "you asked me for an interview and I gave it to you, now I'm asking you for one, surely you owe it to me". So I agreed to return the following day.

The next day, with very little preliminary talk, he asked me whether I thought I could be a Command Catering Adviser. I had no idea, not knowing what were the duties. I asked him what the rank would be. "A major", he replied. It seemed preposterous; how could anyone without any training become a major? "Good heavens", I said, "I couldn't be a major". He was triumphant. "There you are", he said, "I told you you were no good; I offer you an important job and now you say you can't do it". Then he became serious, he explained that he had no qualified men, and had to pick people without training, in the hope that they would succeed. He finished by saying that he had picked me. "Sir Isidore", I said, "I can't cook". "I know you can't", he replied, "but I think you will be able to do it". He was so straight and so shrewd, I felt flattered that I had survived his steely appraisal and I accepted. A week later I was at the Army Catering Corps training depot at Aldershot and within five days I was ordered to report to Northern Command Army head-quarters at York.

It was an ordeal reporting to Northern Command, dressed in the unaccustomed uniform of a second lieutenant and not feeling the part. The Catering Corps was established in the Command but the catering adviser was a civilian. The Army Catering Corps was a comparatively new branch of the services that up to then had made little impact. The fact that the Command catering adviser was a civilian made it difficult for him to be effective in a Command run by trained regular staff officers. As far as I could see he seemed to be used as a trouble shooter, but without commissioned rank he was handicapped.

Within a few days of my arrival at Command, one of the officers from "A" branch, looking after personnel, came into our office and said in a cutting tone of voice, "Laughton, you may disguise yourself as a major". I replied, "Very well put, sir" and thought to myself – the sooner I get out of this outfit the better! At the same time as my rank came through, a posting came from the War Office ordering me to report to Scottish Command the following Monday.

The next day, the same officer from "A" branch came into the office and in his cutting tone of voice, and with no explanation said: "Laughton, you can ignore the posting to Scottish Command". It was depressing, as I was keen to go to Scotland and I was equally keen to get out of Northern Command. That Sunday I met a civilian friend in the Station Hotel at York, who lived at York and was accustomed to the ways of the military command. He noticed that I was depressed and asked me the reason. I told him of my posting to Scotland and of the order to ignore it. "Why don't you go and see the general?" he asked. The suggestion alarmed me. "He is not a bad chap", he said, "they are all much the same; after all he is only a man – go and see him".

Command on a Sunday morning was like other large offices, with few people about except the cleaners. Fortunately the major-general in charge of administration was in his office, so I asked if I could see him. On any other day but Sunday there would have been little chance, but this time I was lucky. It didn't feel like luck when I was shown in – he might be only a man but he looked like a very special sort of man. "The War Office has posted me to Scotland", I told him, "Yes, I know", he replied, "but we want you to stay here". "Well sir, I want to go to Scotland", I said. "Whatever for? Scotland is only a second class command, Northern is a first class command". I could only reply, "I want to go to Scotland, sir". He looked at me with amazement and after a long pause he said, "All right, bugger off". I didn't get any medals for bravery during my military service but I earned one during that interview.

I rushed back to my hotel, packed and leapt into my car and landed up at the North British Hotel, Edinburgh, in time for dinner. The North British is a splendid hotel, large but not too large, built in the days when buildings had style and it had been developed by a railway company with a character of its own. I was given a spacious bedroom overlooking Princes Street gardens, with a magnificent antique bathroom attached. The bath was surrounded by gleaming valves that looked as though they had been made to be operated by the chief engineer of the railway company.

From the moment I drove out of York my spirits had lifted. Crossing the Scottish border north of Berwick I could have shouted for joy. Now in the North British Hotel and feeling at home, I settled down to dinner wondering what Scotland had in store for me.

CHAPTER XV

WITH SCOTTISH COMMAND

Serving in Scottish Command was like serving at the headquarters of a foreign army. The orders came from London, but if the Scotsmen did not approve they would ignore them and work out their own alternative. This was done in many directions; clearly, Scottish Command had its own way of doing things. To start with, although it was a second class command, the General Officer Commanding, General Sir Charles Grant, was a full general, and a Scotsman. His wife, Lady Sybil Grant, was a sister of the Earl of Rosebery and on the Command staff there were a number of Scottish aristocrats.

One of my first consultants was Lady Sybil Grant; she was the president of the command canteen, where they were having a good deal of difficulty. When she heard of my appointment she came in to see whether I could do anything to help. I looked into it and found that the difficulties were mainly caused by the irregular attendance of the voluntary staff. I suggested that a foundation staff of paid workers should be engaged and this solved the problem. Lady Sybil was grateful for my assistance and, realising that I was alone, invited me to spend Christmas day at her home.

It was a fair sized party and after dinner we played charades. I was given a team to lead consisting of Lady Sybil, a young girl, and myself. In one charade we tried to represent the story of Grace Darling, the life-boat heroine, attempting to rescue a lighthouse keeper. I turned myself into a boat and was rowed across the carpet by the girl towards Lady Sybil, who was standing in a corner with a lampshade on her head. She made a splendid lighthouse! There were one or two young officers from Command in the party. The following day the word had gone round that I had turned the general's wife into a lighthouse. The story rescued me from obscurity and made the new department known throughout Command headquarters.

The feeding of the troops was one of the responsibilities of Lieutenant-Colonel Maitland-Dougal. The Colonel was a regular staff officer with several medals for gallantry. He was a well bred Scotsman, a distinguished man with a lively imagination. My arrival seemed to intrigue him; he made me welcome and did everything he could to help me to become effective.

Cries of distress were coming from all quarters of Scotland, there were many new units billeted in every kind of accommodation, derelict mills and factories, empty schools, empty country houses and outbuildings. Most of them had very little cooking equipment, practically no trained cooks and no trained messing officers. I was sent out in response to some of the more desperate calls, to allow me to see the nature of the problems rather than to attempt to solve them.

There was only one long-term solution — training. It was going to be a part of my function to organise training centres for cooks and for messing officers, to set up training courses, and to arrange for a steady intake of trainees to keep the courses filled. It was a considerable task, but no obstacles were put in my way. A chain of training schools covering the Command was rapidly constructed, and I was given sufficient staff to enable me to keep them at full strength.

The difficulty was that the orders from the War Office did not provide for the training schools to be adequately equipped, neither did they provide for sufficient staff in the catering adviser's office to keep them filled to capacity. When I pointed these matters out to Colonel

Maitland-Dougal he encouraged me to make a case for the additional equipment and for the staff that I thought would be required. "Write a clear-cut, cogent memorandum", he said, "but don't let any over-statements creep in — if you do it will be thrown out".

He was right, for if a better way could be found, the Scots would adopt it, if only for the pleasure of beating England to it. The Scottish training centres were given a better specification and I was given an adequate staff, so that when the centres were completed they were kept filled. I was told that the number of trained catering staff being produced in Scotland was exceptionally good. The numbers were sufficiently good to attract the attention of Sir Isidore. He decided to pay Scotland a visit to find out what was going on.

Sir Isidore was a sceptic. He seemed to have come to Scotland with the view that our figures were probably wrong, and that he was the man who was going to puncture them. He would take nothing on trust; all statements were questioned, and it seemed as though he was determined to discredit me. He found out that I had a larger staff than had been authorised by the War Office; how had I got them and why? The answer was easy, I had been able to convince Scottish Command that the War Office authorisation was inadequate.

When he went to the training centres he spotted that they were better equipped than usual, and he noticed that there was a butchery department, again unauthorised. He wanted to know why. I told him that the meat was issued to the large units in carcases and that men needed training as to how to break up the carcases. He noticed that the men working in the butchery were wearing butchers' aprons. He pounced on this — unauthorised again. "Yes", I told him, "unauthorised but necessary".

He stayed for three days and all the time he continued to probe and cross question. I began to feel that as soon as he was back in London I should get my marching orders.

I wondered if there would be any chance of my being accepted as a second lieutenant in the Green Howards. He returned on the sleeper train to London. We had dinner together at the North British, and even at dinner he seemed to be goading me to cross swords with him. When it was time for him to leave I accompanied him down in the hotel lift and along the stark basement corridors of the hotel which lead to the station platforms. I saw him on to the train, thinking that it was probably the last time that I should see him. He put his foot on the railway carriage step and, turning to me, delivered his knock-out blow. "Goodbye, Laughton", he said, "you are doing a first class job up here".

Now that the training courses were established, it was possible to give practical help to units in catering trouble. The capability of the messing officers and the cooks could be assessed and, if necessary, arrangements made for replacements or for further training.

Travelling round the country the distances covered were so great, and the hours I had to put in so long, that I managed to break down the Command rule that staff officers should only be driven by women drivers of the F.A.N.Y. corps. I was allocated a Royal Army Service Corps driver, Private Cuthbertson. He drove my car, which was a large Buick coupé I had bought from an American film technician at Elstree during my film days. It was a flashy car but an extremely good one. There was very little traffic on the roads, so that I discovered the beauties of Scotland under the most favourable conditions, travelling all over by car, from the Borders to the remote Highlands. Cuthbertson was a fishing ghillie from the Borders. When he discovered that I fished, he persuaded me to send for rods which we carried in the car. Spurred on by Cuthbertson, I fished water in many places without authority, the only criterion being that the water looked promising and that there was no one about.

A special call came into headquarters for increased rations for the Independent Companies that were training in the area spread along the road to the Isles from Fort William to Mallaig. The Independent Companies were later to be renamed the Commandos. The training was extremely arduous, so strenuous that ordinary rations would not satisfy their hunger. I was dispatched to Lochailort, where the Brigadier in command had his headquarters, to make a report on the application. On the way from Edinburgh I happened to be reading *Revolt in the Desert* by T. E. Lawrence, in which he described the operations of his small desert force engaged in raiding the German-held Baghdad railway. He had trained his men to exist on chapattis and water, so they were able to carry a month's rations for themselves on the withers of their camels. There was no supply depot and there were no supply lines for the enemy to attack. Lawrence attributed his success to the mobility his force was able to achieve through the simplicity of their supply arrangements.

I spent the night at a small inn at the head of Glenfinnan. After supper, probably at the instigation of Cuthbertson, the proprietor invited me to take one of his boats to troll for sea trout in Loch Shiel. I accepted, and with Cuthbertson taking the oars we fished the head of the loch. It was a lovely evening and a successful one, as we came ashore with five sea trout weighing seventeen pounds — the largest a six-pounder. The innkeeper was delighted with the addition to his larder.

The following morning I arrived at Kinlochailort at the head of Loch Ailort, the headquarters of the Independent Companies. Going in I passed a familiar face, so familiar that I thought I knew him. It was David Niven; I only knew his face through seeing it on the screen.

The commanding officer, a very tough-looking brigadier, was expecting me. He explained the need for extra rations. The training involved climbing mountains, carrying boats, ammunition, assault equipment, and travelling long distances to strike at distant objectives. The men were arriving back at their company headquarters famished. It was impossible to satisfy them with the standard rations. I asked the brigadier whether when they were in action there would be a supply column. "Good heavens, no", he replied, "in action they will carry everything with them". Revolt in the Desert was in my mind. I put it to the brigadier that if the men were to campaign without a supply column, surely it would be necessary to train them to live on simple and transportable rations and to teach them to live off the land. He was sufficiently impressed to ask me to explain. I pointed out that the country they were training in was bursting with supplementary rations, deer, wild goat, salmon, sea trout, brown trout, grouse – all neglected, as sport was at a standstill. I suggested that an expert on the provisioning of polar expeditions should be consulted to see if pemmican and other concentrated foods could be made use of; the brigadier was impressed. He asked me where I had received my training in military tactics. I had to admit that I had had no training. If I had been more honest, I should have lent him my copy of Lawrence's book. As a result of my visit, the application for increased rations was withdrawn and I heard later that the natural resources of the district were made full use of.

Discussing the general messing situation with Colonel Maitland-Dougal, I suggested that as the power in each unit lay in the hands of the commanding officer, it was he who needed practical knowledge of catering, as he was the one who could make effective use of it. The Colonel agreed and asked if I had anything in mind. My suggestion was a two days' messing course for commanding officers. He was impressed by the idea and immediately adopted it. He was so keen on the project that a date had to be fixed. He would have liked it to be in four weeks' time, and I had difficulty in persuading him to put it back to six weeks. The next thing I knew was that he had issued an order that all commanding officers in Scottish Command must attend a two days' messing course, with the date of the first course fixed. The order was greeted with derision throughout the Command.

I knew I was up against it and at that stage, although I was confident the idea was good, I was apprehensive as to whether it could be carried out effectively. The overall idea was based on the old saying: "It's the master's eye that makes the horse grow fat" – which is only true if the master's eye knows what to look for. In this case it was the commanding officers who were the masters, and the object of the course was to make their interest in the quality and quantity of their men's food more effective. The course was an entirely new idea and in all probability it would have to be given to hostile audiences. Many of those attending would be keen perceptive men, consequently the lectures and demonstrations would have to be severely practical. It would be a bit like lecturing to a group of Sir Isidore Salmons all ready to pounce on anything inaccurate or impractical.

With these considerations in mind I set to work. I enlisted the help of Lieutenant Quartermaster Briginshaw, a young catering instructor whom I considered to be the best catering instructor in the Command. We planned the course together. I wrote the lectures and in doing so realised that I must have a practical grip of everything on which I was going to speak. Sir Isidore's stricture when I told him I couldn't cook came back to me. "What, you can't cook? You're no good". There was nothing else for it. I should have to be able to cook all the simple dishes that were going to be lectured on and demonstrated.

Briginshaw had been a first class chef in civil life – I became his pupil in the demonstration kitchen at Glencorse barracks. We cooked brown stew, hot pot, Irish stew, shepherd's pie, steak and kidney pie, rissoles, steamed suet puddings, porridge and every kind of roast, night after night for the best part of a month. During the day I was writing the course and setting up the organisation. The place selected was the cooks' training centre at Glencorse barracks, where there was a suitable small lecture hall and a good demonstration kitchen that would accommodate the twenty officers who were to attend each course.

The general in command of administration, Major-General Gale, was new to the Command. He was intrigued by the idea. He decided to open the first course and directed that it should be attended by the regimental depot commanders. There could not have been a more formidable audience, all bemedalled regulars — experienced veterans. The general briefly introduced himself, declared his faith in the value of the course and left me to it.

It was a fantastic situation — an imitation major lecturing to hard-bitten, experienced, regular soldiers. All I could do was to tell them that I knew it, and ask them to correct me every time I dropped a brick. I stumbled through as best I could, with the backing of excellent demonstrations put on by picked staff, ably supervised by Briginshaw. At the end of the course the Colonel of the Scots Greys drew me aside, "You seem nervous, Laughton", he said, "you needn't be, this is one of the most useful courses that I have ever attended". He went on to ask me to inspect the messing at his regimental barracks and made a date for the following week.

When I turned up at the barracks the colonel was there to meet me and he accompanied me on the tour of inspection. Everything was spot on, the sergeant cook, a smart man impeccably turned out with his staff in spotless whites. All departments were in good order, and great play had been made with white scouring stone with which a white band had been laid round the important pieces of cooking equipment. The *pièce de résistance* was the swill yard where each swill bin was surrounded by a white scoured circle. I regarded the row of bins with dazed astonishment, the sergeant cook stood by with a look of conscious virtue. I had an inspiration. "Sergeant, turn out one of the bins", I said to him. It seemed sacrilege to strew the spotless floor with kitchen waste but it was done. It was the usual kitchen waste, a depressing sight, but there was one unusual feature. At the bottom of the bin was a long cylindrical loosely wrapped parcel. I picked up the parcel, unwrapped it and showed it to the colonel. "What is it?" he asked. "It's a fillet of beef, sir", I said. The other bins were turned out and in them were several parcels each containing choice cuts of meat. "Wash them off, sergeant, and return them to the larder", I said. That was the end of the inspection.

Over a pre-luncheon sherry the colonel asked me to explain. "What does it mean?" he asked and "How did you know?". The meaning was simple. The civilian swill contractor was in collusion with someone on the barracks staff to rob the men of a portion of their rations and this was probably a daily event. As to how I knew — I didn't — but during the inspection I had had the feeling that I was being subjected to a powerful dose of eyewash. The white circles round the bins were the last straw, and it brought to my mind that swill bins were a known receptacle for carrying stolen rations. I think finally it was the look of triumphant virtue on the sergeant's face that triggered me into action.

The two-day courses became progressively more enjoyable. After the strain of the first one, I was more at ease; and as there was a course every fortnight I was able to work on them to build up their effectiveness. In demonstrating the need for the master's eye, I pointed out that the best food in the world is produced by the chef proprietors of France, and by intelligent housewives in the home. In following up this point I asserted that the best food in Scotland was produced by a chef proprietor, Mr.

Heptinstall of the Fortingall Hotel, near Aberfeldy. I had visited his hotel and found a kindred spirit — he was a Yorkshireman. He produced excellent food and he had a very good wine cellar. The war had made his hotel very quiet, but my fortnightly lectures were a remarkable stimulus to his business especially after the course for the Polish commanding officers whose units were quartered in the Perth area and within easy distance of Aberfeldy. As soon as the Poles knew about the Fortingall Hotel they became Mr. Heptinstall's best customers.

Overall the course was successful in stimulating interest in food, partly by demonstrating that army rations could produce very good meals. It convinced the commanding officers that their practical interest would be the most effective weapon to improve the feeding of their men. It helped them to weigh up the quality of their catering personnel so that the good ones could be encouraged by appreciation, further training, and promotion. Most important it helped them to recognise lazy and incompetent work and to be able to spot the signs of pilfering and dishonesty.

At each course there was always one or two outstanding men. The dedicated professional soldier is a most impressive man, and they were to be found not only amongst the regulars, but also amongst the men serving for the duration of the war. Such men welcomed anything that would assist them in looking after the welfare of their men. Between the fortnightly courses I was moving round the Command, and I found how much the course was being appreciated. It was remarkable how effective it was proving. Apart from my own observations, this was pointed out to me by Major-General Gale whose remedy, if he came across a unit with defective messing, was to arrange for the commanding officer to attend the next course.

I was taking my leaves back at home, staying with

mother at the Pavilion or fishing in the Highlands. I had made arrangements for a fishing leave when I had a telephone call from my brother Frank. He wanted me to get home as quickly as possible but he would not say why. Reluctantly I cancelled the arrangements for the fishing trip and set off for home. A day or so before Frank had telephoned, a chauffeur had arrived at the hotel and had asked for Mr. Laughton. Frank had come forward. The chauffeur handed him a new motor-car log book saying: "Your Rolls is at the door, sir". And there it was, a brand-new Rolls Royce. To Frank's relief, the log book was made out in my name. He directed the chauffeur to deliver the car to me at the North British Hotel, Edinburgh — but he refused. He left the log book with Frank and took the train back to London. Frank had the car sheeted up in a garage and sent for me.

It was a present from Madge; she had always been unpredictable — this time she had excelled herself. I went to look at it, but I felt dreadful. I had the feeling that it was a despairing gesture from an unhappy woman. We had been happy together, but we had not the courage to live together permanently. I don't know what lay behind the present of the car because I never saw her again. Sometime later a letter arrived from her husband's solicitors. The car was unused; I had not even sat in it. Eventually, I sold it and put the proceeds in a separate bank account. It was a relief to send them the cheque.

I had been in Scottish Command for close on two years when I received a telephone call from Sir Isidore. He wanted to know whether I would be prepared to organise a new government corporation to be named the "National Service Hostels' Corporation". "What is a hostel?", I asked him. "I can't tell you over the telephone" he said, "but I consider I am offering you the spot catering job". I hesitated. I was very happy in Scotland. I loved the country, I liked the Scottish regulars and I was enjoying working in

Scottish Command. "It is a very important job", Sir Isidore said. "I'm sure it is", I replied, "but I think what I am doing now is important". There was a pause, then back he came in his natural form, "Why will you always argue with me, my boy? Come to London, and I'll tell you all about it".

When I got to London he explained that the Ministry of Labour was about to set up a government financed corporation to run hostels to accommodate civilian workers all over the country. The workers were to be directed by the Ministry away from their homes under the powers of the National Service Act. The Minister of Labour, Ernest Bevin, had asked Sir Isidore to recommend a man to organise and run the corporation, and he had recommended me. "But, Sir Isidore", I said, "I don't know anything about hostels". "I know you don't", he replied, "and you didn't know anything about army catering, you couldn't even cook but you have managed". I hastened to tell him that now I could cook, he brushed that aside. "Well, my boy, will you do it?". I had to accept — there was something about him that made it impossible to refuse.

CHAPTER XVI

THE NATIONAL SERVICE
HOSTELS' CORPORATION

The move from Edinburgh to London was the beginning
of a testing time. Two years in Scotland, without my
accustomed social life in the hotel, had made me realise
that I was a lonely man ready for marriage. I was thirty-
eight years of age, and because of my philandering, I had
blunted my instincts and lost my judgement. I married
a charming young girl of good family and we set up
house together in Hadley Wood, close to the home of
her parents.

Within a week of our marriage, we both realised that we
were hopelessly incompatible. In four months we parted.
She joined the forces and I moved to Stanmore. The four
months had been a terrible time, not only at home but
also at my work.

The National Service Hostels' Corporation was a new
type of government operation, the brain child of Ernest
Bevin. It was a corporation working outside the Civil
Service, created to carry out ministerial policy, but,
although outside the Civil Service, it was in reality controlled by civil servants. When I arrived at the offices
I found a financial director had been installed, R. H. Bindloss, an ex-deputy financial director of the Ministry of
Labour. He had the sterling qualities of a top grade British
civil servant together with some of their faults. He seemed
to me like a man straight out of the pages of *Dombey and
Son*. He informed me that he was usually known as
"R. H. B." and that he thought in view of my position as
managing director it would be appropriate for him to call
me "governor". He took me under his wing and proceeded

to instruct me in the ways of the Civil Service, both in the office and outside; outside by taking me to lunch daily at his club — the National Liberal — where I could absorb the ambiance of the Civil Service world.

I learnt from R. H. B. how many things there were that just must not be done and the necessity to hasten slowly, very slowly. To him the Hostels' Corporation was a Ministerial foible that would probably never become a reality. As far as we were concerned, we had been created to do a job that might never materialise; above all, we must see that we should never be a nuisance to our creators. When I tried to discuss with him the task that lay ahead of us, he would say: "Don't worry, governor, there may never be any hostels".

Day by day, I became increasingly frustrated. Whilst R. H. B. was happy to lie fallow, devoting his time to making sure that I did not put my foot in it, I began to feel that I must get back to the army. I received an invitation from Sir Isidore to have supper with him in a suite at the Cumberland Hotel as he wanted to know how I was getting on. He had laid on a small buffet in the apartment so that we could help ourselves without interruption. I told him of my frustration owing to the lack of action, and that it was like living in a world of blotting paper.

I told him of the Board of Directors: the chairman, Lord Rushcliffe — an ex-Minister of Labour; Margaret Bondfield — another ex-Minister of Labour; Harry Methven — an industrialist and a friend of Ernest Bevin; they were a front to a world of inaction. If it was to go on like this I was determined to get out, and to get back to the army. He was very concerned; he assured me that the Minister had told him that the corporation had a very big job to do, so he advised me to go to the top to find out the position. He finished by asking me to promise not to resign without further consultation with him.

The following day I told R. H. B. that I was not

satisfied, and that I intended to go to the Ministry. He seemed to think it unwise, but he agreed that the man to see was Godfrey Ince, the Director of Manpower. I made an appointment to see him that afternoon. He seemed astonished at my lack of information. When I told him of R. H. B.'s dictum, "Don't worry, governor, there may never be any hostels", he laughed, recognising the true man of masterly inaction. Before I left his office I had found out that hostels to accommodate about thirty thousand residents were in course of construction, some of them due to be finished in about two months' time. As each one was finished, the corporation would be expected to take them over and run them; and this was only a start – many more were in the pipeline.

I was appalled. We were totally unprepared, with no foundation organisation apart from myself, Mr. Bindloss and one or two junior civil servants. Godfrey Ince took me to Sir Thomas Phillips, the Permanent Secretary, who asked me whether I had a plan for the organisation ready. I had no plan because up to then I had had no information, so he suggested that I should work on it, and come back in a week's time to let him know my requirements.

All that I then knew was that the hostels would be utility hotels, each accommodating from four hundred to one thousand residents. The ones that we now knew about were situated in Coventry, Reading, Corsham and Cumberland, and I was told that in course of time they would cover almost every industrial area. Some of them would be isolated, and in view of their large capacity they would have to provide entertainment as well as food and sleeping accommodation. The operation would have to be departmentalised; so, mostly out of my imagination, I prepared a memorandum setting out the Head Office requirements, basing it on the assumption that within six months the corporation would be accommodating approximately fifty thousand residents.

For the next meeting with Sir Thomas I took Bindloss with me. The meeting was held round the conference table in his office, and Sir Thomas had brought in all his heads of departments. My memorandum envisaged a comprehensive staff to cover all the departments I thought necessary. In addition to accountancy, catering, personnel and purchasing I had added a Welfare and Entertainments department, also a shop organiser and an architect. When I finished, Sir Thomas asked for comments. The only items questioned were the ones concerning the shops and the architect; but after my explanations they were both accepted.

The outcome of the meeting was that the plan for the organisation was endorsed and I was given the go-ahead. R. H. B. looked a little stunned; walking back to our office he expressed his feelings: "You are in a mess now, governor, they have given you all you asked for — now you have no excuses".

On the contrary, it was salvation for me. I was on the verge of a nervous collapse; the breakdown of my marriage and the period of frustration at the office had all but put me over the edge. Now, the intense activity pulled me back.

Whilst the build-up of the staff was proceeding, I had to tour the country to see the hostels in course of construction. The hostels were being built by the Ministry of Works, and I toured them in company with the architect responsible for their planning and construction. Seeing them only partially constructed was sufficient to drive home the special nature of the problem. They were built on spacious campus sites around a central block, which consisted of entrance hall, offices, dining hall, lounges, writing room and large recreation hall equipped with a proscenium stage, the blocks of sleeping accommodation radiated round the central block. A hostel was designed to house a self-contained community.

Each hostel would need a manager, an accounts officer, a caterer, a housekeeper, an entertainments officer, a nurse in charge of the sick bay and a shopkeeper to run what would amount to a village store. How it was to be run would have to be expressed in a code of management, which I should have to think out and write. This would have to be done in time for the opening of the first hostel, scheduled to be in about two months' time. I had to visualise the operation of running a hostel, splitting it into departments, define the duties of each department, and decide the number of staff that would be required. Having done this, I had to persuade the Ministry of Works to provide appropriate staff accommodation. I wanted a small bungalow for each manager and a comfortable bed-sitting room for each departmental head. I had to struggle to get these. Good accommodation proved to be one of the major factors in helping us to build up a staff of over twelve thousand in under two years. It was a period of intense activity. I had no one to whom I could delegate the writing of the general management codes; there was no precedent, and nobody with any conception of what was involved. For two months I had to work impossible hours, drafting and redrafting, until at last the management code was ready for the first group of hostels. I had a marvellous secretary, Miss Mabel Griffiths, who worked alongside me and never grumbled however long the hours.

The original idea for the Hostels' Corporation had been Ernest Bevin's, so that it was not surprising that soon after the first hostels were opened for residents he went to have a look at one. He was not disappointed. He quickly sensed the atmosphere and, with his friendly approach, he was able to draw out of the residents their feelings about hostel life. He hated formality; it was in places like the hand laundry, the sick bay, or at the hostel shop counter that he made his contacts. His impressions were good and he came away satisfied that his intentions

The Royal Hotel

The Royal's Galleried Staircase

Esme and Tom Laughton, 1947, with a morning's catch of
three tunny, weighing 2028 pounds

Mrs. Constable Asleep, by John Constable
(One of my favourite paintings)

in setting up the corporation were being carried out.

I came to know Bevin well. One of the hostel corporation's directors, Harry Methven, the industrialist, was his friend. He entertained Bevin frequently, and I was often included in the party. On one of Bevin's visits to the north he stayed with us at the Pavilion, where he got on very well with mother. I took him to lunch at my house alongside the Royal. I thought he would enjoy drinking a very fine Grand Montrachet, vintage 1929, which he certainly did! He commented, "I don't know what you call this, Tom. I call it bottled sunshine". On another occasion he brought his wife to stay with us at the farm at Lockton. Harry Methven and his wife were in the party. I had managed to obtain a home-fed, home-cured, Yorkshire ham off the ration. Harry was struck by the delicious flavour and asked me how on earth I had been able to get hold of it. Bevin answered for me, "Don't ask bloody silly questions, Harry", he said.

Ernest was a delightful guest — relaxed, appreciative and such good company. He was always interesting with stories of his past life, incisive comments on the present, and at his best when his lively mind was looking to the future. He was a confirmed European and when he talked of the future of Europe I gained the impression that he looked forward to a European federation of nations. I believe that had he become Prime Minister in place of Attlee, he would have led Great Britain into becoming a founder member of the European Common Market.

Now that he had created the corporation and approved of the way it was operating, he was constantly finding new tasks for it to do, and explaining to me what he had in mind. He was determined to use his power for the good of the country, in particular for the good of the workers. Bevin had an intimate knowledge of the docks, he knew there were seamen's hostels, but he did not approve of them. He thought that a seamen's hostel should give relief from the drab surroundings of dockland, and that they should be situated at the centre of the city. When he decided to set up a chain of hostels in all the main ports he sent for me, expounded his ideas and then gave his orders.

The Glasgow seamen's hostel was financed by American money. When it was ready it was opened by Mr. Winant, the American Ambassador, and the opening was attended by Bevin. In the course of the opening I had to make a speech. That evening Bevin sent for me to go to his sitting room in the hotel. He had been impressed by my speech, "You ought to go into parliament", he said, "I will arrange for you to stand for one of the seats financed by my Union". "But Minister", I said, "I am not a socialist". "Oh yes you are", he said, "you are a socialist all right – a practical one". He returned to the idea several times, but I never felt ready to take it further.

Bevin's interest in the corporation was valuable. It enabled me to fight the Ministry of Works to obtain workable standards of planning and construction. The main concern of the Ministry of Works was to save building labour and building materials. If they had had their way, the standards of the hostels would have been reduced until they became unworkable. Ernest Bevin was the most powerful Minister in the government apart from Winston Churchill, so with his backing I was able to insist that the standards were kept to a workable minimum.

The Ministry of Aircraft Production was one of the Ministries for which the corporation worked. At one period, the Minister was Sir Stafford Cripps. I received a summons to go to see him. One of the hostels housing aircraft workers was run by Butlin's under a management agreement made with his Ministry. The hostel was situated near to his home and was apparently causing scandal. He informed me that in his area it was known as "Butlin's brothel". I wondered if he had made allowance for the temptations of alliteration. He had been round the hostel in company with a local bishop, and with his own eyes had observed French letters on the hostel pavements. I attempted to register becoming shock. The Minister retailed other items of gossip. In an unguarded moment I said to him: "But Minister, you must have some regard for the laws of evidence". I had gone too far. He looked at me with a petrifying gaze. "What", he said, "You are telling *me* about the laws of evidence?" I said no more, and the outcome was that the corporation had to take the hostel over.

As we were running a considerable number of hostels for his Ministry, Sir Stafford became interested and visited some of them. Sometime later, I received an invitation to lunch from Lady Cripps. Over coffee she told me that Stafford could not understand why Bevin treated him as he did. She went on to say that Stafford had a great admiration for Ernest. He considered that Ernest had done more practical good for the working men than any other politician; she finished by saying that Stafford would follow him anywhere.

The following weekend Bevin was lunching with Harry Methven at his riverside house at Henley and I was invited. After lunch Bevin and I were walking beside the river, so I took the opportunity to deliver Stafford's message. Bevin listened with attention and walked along digesting it. When he did speak he said, "Yes, I believe he would follow me", and then continued, "Do you know what's the trouble with him?" "No", I said. "It's his conscience", he continued, "Stafford is the sort of chap who will meet colleagues to discuss a problem: if a solution is arrived at, and a plan of action agreed, Stafford goes away convinced. Then in the night he gets a message direct from God and all is changed; that's his bloody conscience".

It was the realism of Bevin that made it difficult for him to get on with men such as Stafford Cripps. Bevin was no doctrinaire socialist. He did not regard the successful industrialist as an enemy, but rather as an ally who could

help him to get the improved living conditions for the
working men for which he was striving. The man he could
not stand was the financial manipulator, the entrepreneur.
One of his pet hates was Lord Beaverbrook; he could
neither understand nor approve the influence that Beaverbrook had on Churchill.

It was Bevin's powerful position in the government that
held back Beaverbrook's influence. Churchill was constantly pressing to advance Beaverbrook; he wanted to
make him his deputy Prime Minister. During the crucial
days of the war it was out of the question, for Churchill
knew that in those days the co-operation of the socialists
was vital, and that the advancement of Beaverbrook was
likely to wreck it. It was towards the end of the war, when
the allies had gained the upper hand, that Churchill
thought himself powerful enough to make the move. Bevin
told me that in this period he was sent for by Churchill
and informed that he was about to make Beaverbrook his
deputy. "When?", asked Bevin. "Why do you want to
know?" asked Churchill. "Because", Bevin had replied,
"the day he comes in, I go out". Churchill lost his temper
and went round the room kicking the furniture.

In addition to politicians the work brought me into
contact with other prominent people. The hostels covered
a wide section of interests. One of the premises run by the
corporation was the Merchant Navy Club, Rupert Street,
from which was broadcast a lively weekly radio programme. The club was visited by the King and Queen, and
it fell to me to escort the King round the premises.

Not long after this I had to take him round the Leave
Club for young Dominion officers in Grosvenor Street.
This club had been converted from the town mansion of
Sir Ernest Cassel. The King, noticing the opulence, said to
me, "I hope these young men don't think this is a typical
example of English taste". One thing that seemed to
revolt him was the bath in the owner's suite, which was in

the form of a solid silver shell let into a marble floor.

Not long after, I went to an investiture at the palace to receive the O.B.E. I marched up a sloping gangway to the level platform to face the King before stepping a pace forward to be given the decoration. The King looked up at me and said in a very quiet voice, "What, you again?" Later I received the C.B.E., this time without comment.

New jobs kept coming in. One was the organisation of a chain of hostels covering every coal-mining district, to accommodate the young men conscripted to the mines under the Bevin Boys scheme. To get some understanding of the working conditions of these young men, I went down a couple of pits. They were both intimidating – a frightening journey down the shaft, at the bottom the ill-lit passages, dripping roofs – a general impression of darkness and discouragement. The ones I explored had extremely low roofs, close to the coal face. I should have hated to work in them. The young men we were accommodating would almost all have preferred to be conscripted to the armed forces so it was not surprising that they were difficult to cope with in the hostels.

The difficulties were anticipated. Extreme care was taken in the selection of hostel managers and in the selection of housekeepers and caterers – especially the caterers, as it was realised that young men doing hard physical work underground were certain to be extremely hungry. I visited one of the Bevin Boy hostels where there was trouble, and where I had been told that nearly all the young residents were communists. When I met the residents' committee I mentioned this; I wanted to make the point that here was a chance to live a successful communal life. When I mentioned the word "communist", the chairman of the committee flared up, "We are not communists", he said, "we are Trotskyites". I did not know the difference, but I did manage to come to an understanding and they undertook to co-operate rather than disrupt the place.

One of our problems was that in dealing with large communities there were no powers of discipline to maintain reasonable behaviour. All that could be done was to refuse to accommodate those residents who behaved badly. In well run hostels, discipline was maintained by the residents' committee. There was a residents' committee in every hostel. It was an essential part of management technique to gain the confidence of this committee so that its co-operation was ensured. In cases where the ejection of a resident was called for, it was always desirable to have the agreement of the committee. When we ran into difficulty it was generally through neglect of the democratic technique.

One of the hardest tasks was the organisation of hostels for the sudden influx into London of the bomb-damage repair workers. Thousands of labourers were poured into London to knock down and tidy up the sites of hundreds of badly damaged buildings. To accommodate these men a large number of Gibraltarians, who had been living in requisitioned hotels, were sent back home, and the hotels were taken over to accommodate the influx. The Gibraltarians had catered for themselves, but we had to set up a full hostel service for the new occupiers. In addition to the hotels, a large number of the mansions in Onslow Square were taken over, and a huge canteen was erected in the Onslow Square gardens.

The decision to import the workers and to take over the hotels was taken so rapidly that it was impossible to recruit sufficient staff in time to run them. Somebody had the idea of appealing for temporary help to the provincial domestic science colleges. They all responded willingly. Each one sent a team of girls, and each team was allocated to one of the large hotels. In every case the Gibraltarians had left the premises in a filthy state. The girls worked magnificently, cleaning the kitchens in time for the arrival of the bomb-damage repair workers. Every team produced food that satisfied the men until the time came when we were able to replace them. It was a relief to see them leave London, as this was the time of the flying bombs. Fortunately, there were no casualties and they all returned home safely.

By this time the Hostels' Corporation had opened well over two hundred hostels of many different kinds; it was employing over twelve thousand staff, and it was accommodating over one hundred thousand residents. The expansion had taken place in a little over three years.

CHAPTER XVII

BACK AT THE ROYAL

In the spring of 1944 I met Esmé Holliday, a beautiful young woman from Scarborough who was serving as an officer in the W.R.N.S. We had known each other at home, but in a period when I was wasting my time philandering. She was tall, with chestnut hair, grey-blue eyes, a lovely skin, fine features and a striking high-spirited carriage. She looked stunning in her naval uniform. She was stationed in London in quarters close to Hyde Park. We saw a great deal of each other, I fell in love with her, and eventually persuaded her to marry me as soon as I became free.

I had married my first wife outside the Catholic church; this time I wanted to be married with the blessing of the church. I went to a Jesuit priest in Farm Street to explain my position. The priest listened to my story; he told me that the church did not regard my first marriage as a sacrament but only as a civil contract, so that once my divorce was through I would be free to be married in the Catholic church.

As soon as my divorce became absolute Esmé and I were married in the Catholic church of St. James, Spanish Place, in January 1945. Our marriage had a disastrous start. Only three days after the wedding, during a brief honeymoon in Brighton, the news came that Esmé was in desperate trouble. I will not record in detail what was involved, but the outcome was public disgrace and our being separated for nearly a year. It was during this period that I discovered anew what a remarkable woman my mother was. She stood by us without flinching. It was her strength that helped me to be strong. It was a dreadful time for Esmé and me, but it was partly through our suffering that a bond of love and respect was created that was to be the strongest influence in our lives together. It was a turning point in my life, and I came out of it a changed man.

My days with the Hostels' Corporation were coming to an end. With the end of the war, thousands of the directed workers were returning home and many of the hostels were emptying. I was in a state of shock. Bindloss, who by now was a friend as well as a colleague, did everything he could to lighten my load.

After the general election in July 1945, Ernest Bevin, the new Foreign Minister, sent for me. He was concerned about the conditions of some of the German civilians, and he was proposing to set up a relief organisation which he wanted me to organise and take charge of. I told him that I was not equal to taking on a new task. I wanted to concentrate on my own problems and to be freed so that I could set up a home with Esmé. Ernest understood and promised to help me. The following day he rang me up; he had been in touch with the Adjutant General and had arranged for my release from the army. "You can go home", he told me, "as soon as your desk is cleared up. Bindloss will take over from you". Within a month I was able to hand over my responsibilities. I bought a beautiful house standing on eight acres of good land at Scalby, three miles outside Scarborough, and when Esmé and I returned to Yorkshire we set up our home there. When we returned home everyone went out of their way to make us welcome. We received a round of invitations, some from people that we scarcely knew. It was a heartening experience.

The hotel was in a shocking condition after the six years of war. I took Esmé to see it and when she saw the conditions at the front of the house and behind, she blenched.

For the first year she was so busy setting up our home that she rarely visited the hotel. It was busy enough but the standards were dreadful and it was a relief to close it down at the end of the season.

During the winter we explored the hotel together. Esmé had been brought up in the hotel business. She realised immediately the magnitude of the task that lay in front of us. "We can't get this right living at Scalby", she said, "we shall have to live in the hotel". So, by the time it re-opened in the following spring, we had moved in.

Esmé's capability was a revelation. She quickly gathered together an effective housekeeping staff, and although the hotel was in a shabby and badly equipped condition, she soon made it sparkle. Our new home in Scalby had a good garden and with it we had inherited an experienced gardener. All the flowers were sent in to the hotel, where they compensated to a certain degree for the drab surroundings. The garden was to become one of the principal features of the hotel, as it enabled us to make lavish use of flowers. It was developed with the needs of the hotel in mind: hot-house plants to fill the jardinière that was a feature of the entrance hall; flowers specially grown to fill the urn that stood facing the hotel entrance; even Christmas roses for the Christmas season. Mrs. Haddon, the hotel florist, became one of the most important members of the staff, working hand in glove with Raymond, the gardener at Scalby.

It was impossible to find a laundry that would launder to standards that would satisfy Esmé. I solved the problem by buying a laundry, thinking that she would take it on as a part of her department. But she jibbed and I had to take it on myself. It was a considerable time before I succeeded in turning out linen that would satisfy her. But we did succeed and the laundry played an important part in preserving our linen and enabling us to use it lavishly.

The war conditions had left behind depressed kitchen

standards. The use of packet soups and gravy browning was accepted; meat was boned, roasted and then allowed to go cold so that it could be cut paper-thin on a meat-slicer to be warmed up and served with ersatz gravy. The chefs had got used to these abominable practices which were easy for them and, in those days of scarcity, accepted by the customers. The chefs resisted my efforts to revert to the sound classical methods of pre-war days. Eventually, I had to take over control, write the menus, follow them up day by day in the kitchens and check the quality of the kitchen output in the food services at the start of every lunch and dinner. It was unorthodox hotel practice; usually the Head Chef is in sole charge of his kitchen and is solely responsible for kitchen standards. The only control exercised by the management being through the figures, which demonstrate the percentage of gross profit that the chef is producing. With my method, I took responsibility for the gross profit percentage and was able to make the quality of the kitchen output the primary consideration.

Whilst Esmé and I were dealing with the day to day running problems, we were faced with the task of bringing back the original interior distinction of the hotel. I had made a start before the war; now the work had to be completed. I established workshops at the back of the hotel and gathered together a team of craftsmen: three cabinet-makers, joiners, electricians and plumbers. The decorators were led by a remarkable foreman, Charlie Waller – not only a skilled decorator, but a delightful man – talented, conscientious and gentle. He became, and still is, one of my best friends.

I sent for John Hill, the London decorator and designer with whom I had worked at the Pavilion. He immediately appreciated the original quality of the interior architecture and everything he did subscribed to it. The task ahead was a glorious opportunity for me to restart my collecting.

Once again I was providing the focal points for John's decorative schemes — this time on a grander scale.

Gradually the hotel was transformed and once the programme of transformation began there was a constant need for chandeliers, fine pieces of furniture, *objets d'art* and paintings. Green and Abbott, John Hill's shop in London, stocked such things and I became one of their best customers. Leslie Boothman, an antique dealer in Scarborough, had a good eye for beautiful things; he became an effective collaborator. In addition to these sources there were country house sales in our area, at which I was able to acquire many fine pieces.

Before the programme was completed I acquired a collection of chandeliers — a set of four from Streatlam Castle, the Bowes Lyon residence; a pair from Hawkhills; a magnificent early eighteenth century chandelier from Hickleton Hall — a Halifax residence — and the principal chandelier from Bath House, Piccadilly. The one from Bath House was hung in the galleried entrance hall, immediately over the place where the double staircase joined and finished in a single flight. The carpet for the hall and staircase was designed by an Italian who had designed the carpet for Covent Garden Opera House and it was carried out in colours selected by John Hill. Where the staircase met, we placed a fine large urn which was kept filled with a succession of flower arrangements — the first thing to be seen on entering the hall. It made as impressive an entrance as any I have known; possibly a little theatrical, but I have always held the view that there is a relationship between hotels and the theatre. I believe that hotels, like the theatre, should be larger than life, and that to enter an hotel should be like entering another world, as one does when the curtain goes up in a theatre.

Scarborough was getting back into its stride as a seaside resort. A most welcome feature was the return of the Fol de Rol company led by its producer, director and writer,

Rex Newman, fresh from his war services with E.N.S.A. He opened for his first post-war season at the small Spa Theatre. Rex was a marvellous picker. He always brought good performers; not established stars but there was always star material amongst them. Charlie, Frank and I had been Fol de Rol fans since our childhood. I believe to this day that Rex Newman's Fol de Rols was the finest seaside entertainment in the world. Amongst the company of his first post-war season was David Nixon and working as his stooge a young man with tremendous personality and talent, Norman Wisdom. They were both unknown but completely dedicated. I was delighted that Rex had come back to Scarborough and I gave several parties for them. The first in the Winston Churchill suite; the star of this party was David, he revelled in close conjuring. Nothing would stop him, an audience of two was sufficient to keep him happy. Subsequent parties were larger, too big for the Churchill suite, so we staged them in the ballroom; here Norman was the star, spending all his time on the band dais, playing drums and saxophones, falling about, living in a riotous world of his own.

I am not a party-giver except when it comes to theatricals. They are the most rewarding of all guests with their capacity to entertain and their capacity to enjoy themselves. We once gave a party to the *Ballet Rambert* company. They were very shy when they arrived. We had prepared a stunning buffet, which at first seemed to outface them, but when they did get going they really set about it. Later in the evening I saw one of the male dancers whirling Madame Rambert round and round at shoulder height in the centre of the dance floor; the party was clearly a success.

We were so busy for the first two years that there was no time to take a holiday, but in the course of our first year back in Scarborough there was a brief interlude. In late August, during a spell of beautiful weather, I had a

telephone call from Tom Pashby, the skipper of the
Our Maggie. He had had reports of tunny being seen by the
herring fishermen fishing north-east of Whitby. He wanted
to know whether I still had my fishing gear and, as I had,
he suggested that we should have another go. We arranged
to sail the following evening. In the meantime I checked
over the gear.

The following evening I joined Tom at the quayside; we
went aboard the *Our Maggie* and set off for the herring
fleet at about 10. 30 p.m. It was a grand feeling being at
sea again, steaming past the Castle Hill and watching the
lights of Scarborough recede, with a flutter of excitement
in my stomach. Tom was steering — as pleased as I was to
be on the tunny hunt again. "It won't be as long this time"
he said, "they were telling me on Saturday that there are
hundreds of tunny about, go below and have a kip — we
shall be fishing as soon as dawn breaks".

I went below and lay down in the creaking smelly
cabin. When I came on deck again, the lights of the herring
fleet were all around us. We were eighteen miles north-
east of Whitby; the sea was calm, the deck lights of the
herring drifters reflected on the water and there were
shadowy figures on the decks preparing for the haul.
"Get your gear on", said Tom, "You'll be fishing soon".
Dawn was breaking as the herring boats began to haul,
whilst we cruised gently amongst the fleet, searching for
a sign of tunny. There were plenty of blow fish about
(small whales that spout a vapour with an oily smell).
Suddenly a boil was spotted, then a tunny fin cut the
surface. The dinghy was hauled alongside, Charlie the boatman took the oars and I scrambled aboard. The rod was
handed down, the butt bolted into the swivelled holder
and we were ready for action. My hook, baited with a
herring, was taken almost at once. My first tunny had
taken over four hours to bring to the gaff; this time I was
more experienced.

There is no stopping the first run of a tunny, it is far too large and powerful, and incredibly fast. The reel screams and the pressure on the point of the rod is so great that the angler can only keep it up by bringing his harness into play so that the strength of his shoulders and the weight of his body are added to the strength of his arms. It is more good luck than skill that is needed in the first few minutes. The vital moment comes when the fish pauses after its first run. It is then that the pressure must be applied by dropping the point of the rod, reeling in the few feet of slack line, and pumping the fish a few feet nearer to the boat by lifting the point of the rod. If the fish is allowed to dwell and get its second wind, it will swim gently away towing the boat behind it, or it will sound to the bottom and after that the struggle can go on for hours. The secret is never to release the pressure, keeping command of the fish by dropping and lifting the point of the rod and reeling in again and again and again. This time the fish made no second run; within an hour, the steel trace was near enough to the top of the rod to allow Charlie to seize it, bring the fish close alongside and bury the gaff in its huge gleaming side. The fish was nearly as long as the boat.

The pressure had been as much on me as on the fish but the excitement had kept me going. I was fishing again before the first tunny had been hauled aboard the *Our Maggie*. Within half an hour I was into another. Again we had it gaffed within the hour. The sun was still low in the sky when I hooked and played the third. We were back in the harbour by mid-day with three fish aboard. I was completely done, my back was aching, my arm muscles throbbing, all I wanted to do was to get into a hot bath. So I made tracks for home, leaving the three huge fish almost covering the deck of the *Our Maggie*.

Later that afternoon the telephone rang; it was Frank Watkinson, the secretary of the tunny club. "You are wanted down at the harbour", he said. "The press want to take your photograph with the three fish". "What do they weigh?", I asked him. "Five hundred and thirty-six pounds, seven hundred and seven pounds and seven hundred and eighty-five pounds". "Good God," I said, "there won't be room for me in the picture". Esmé and I went down and we were photographed with the three fish, together with the Mayor who happened to be my old friend, John Jackson, the local preacher from Burniston. The day's tunny fishing was my only holiday that year. Esmé was engrossed with her new home, and she had no wish to be away.

The following year we were together in the hotel, both frantically busy, too busy to think of taking a break. It was not until the third year that we took our first holiday together. The hotel was taking shape. During the summer it was packed to capacity and running smoothly, so smoothly that I thought I could afford to leave it and take a month away.

Ever since my service in Scottish Command I had had at the back of my mind the intention to re-visit the Western Highlands. I had conceived the idea during a visit to a batallion of the Seaforth Highlanders quartered in and around the Highland Hotel, Strathpeffer, a little spa resort twenty-five miles north of Inverness. In the evening, I had strolled up the hill above the hotel and looked westward. The sun was setting, throwing the hills into a blaze of colour, a marvellous and unforgettable sight. I had determined then that one day I must explore this wonderful country.

A friend of mine, Captain Louis Milloy who had served with me in Scottish Command, had recommended a small hotel on the shore of Loch Maree, so I booked for a stay of four weeks. Loch Maree proved to be more beautiful than I could have imagined. When I first saw it from the head of the pass of Glen Dochartie, it was so magnificent that for a moment my heart stood still. As we drove down the pass towards the Loch, the peak of Slioch mountain came into view. Never had I seen anything finer. I did not anticipate that even here I was to become embroiled in the cares and worries of further hotel-keeping.

CHAPTER XVIII

HALCYON DAYS AT LOCH MAREE

We had booked at the Kinlochewe Lodge Hotel at the eastern end of Loch Maree — a delightful situation but a very badly managed hotel. Our dinner the first night was so impossible that we got up hungry. We took the car up Glen Torridon and on the shores of Loch Torridon we found a croft where the crofters cooked us a meal of bacon and eggs.

Mr. Chisholm, the manager, who knew I was an hotel-keeper, spoke to me the following morning. He confessed that neither he nor his wife knew anything about catering and asked if I would help him. For our own sakes I was glad to do so. The first three days of our holiday I spent most of the time getting to know the cook and weighing up the food resources of the district. Plenty of good food was available, including excellent oatmeal, beautiful fat kippers, an unlimited supply of eggs, and prawns, salmon and sea trout from the Gairloch pier less than twenty miles away. The hotel belonged to a Scottish syndicate, and, as one of the members was a butcher, the meat supply was no problem.

The cook was a poor manager, with no idea of how to compose menus. She was a reasonably competent cook with a limited range and a nice person. She could make good broths, she was a fair roast cook, she could make good Scottish sweets and she was a good baker. We got on well. Within three days the food was good enough for anybody.

Mr. and Mrs. Chisholm were relieved; they could not do enough for us. Mr. Chisholm arranged for me to have an excellent ghillie, Alister Mathieson, who was primarily a stalker. He knew so much that it was a joy going up the hill with him. He had the eye of a hawk and he quietly pointed out many things that were completely new to me. To be with such a man was in itself an experience. He knew the haunts of the golden eagle, the peregrine falcon, the buzzards, and he took me to a remote loch high up on the hill where there was a pair of red-throated divers with their young. His eye could pick out the red deer grazing on a distant slope. When I told him I had never seen a ptarmigan, we made an expedition to the high slopes where we came across them.

It was a wonderful holiday, fishing the remote lochs and climbing the shoulder of Slioch mountain to fish Loch Garbaig on its northern side. On a hot brilliant day, when it was useless to fish for anything else, we went fishing for pike on Loch Roshke. We brought back sixty pounds of pike; the boot of the car was full. Donald Urquhart, a stonemason, working in the yard behind the hotel, came to inspect the catch. He was later to become our ghillie at the Loch Maree Hotel, where we fished together for over twenty years.

We stayed at the Kinlochewe Lodge for two years running, but the third year we moved ten miles further down the loch to the Loch Maree Hotel. Loch Maree is a narrow loch about seventeen miles long and a mile and a quarter wide at its widest point. Half way down the loch there is a cluster of islands around which are the best holding grounds for sea trout, which in Loch Maree run up to over twenty pounds in weight. The islands teem with wild life — red deer, roe deer, wild goat, otters, black-throated divers, grey lag geese, ravens, buzzards, peregrine falcon, merlin and kestrel. There is not a sign of habitation except for one or two ruins, and one beautiful shooting lodge, Letterewe, like a small French chateau situated on the northern slope of the loch and only accessible by boat from a jetty on the southern shore.

On the southern shore, half way down the loch facing the islands, is the Loch Maree Hotel, a small hotel built in 1872 to accommodate anglers. When we were staying at Kinlochewe Lodge we would go down in the evening to visit the Loch Maree Hotel, partly for a drive along the shores of the loch but mainly to see the catches of sea trout laid out in the hall of the hotel. Laid out on trays the fish were an astonishing sight — fresh run, gleaming like polished platinum, sometimes as many as eighty fish. It was no wonder that it was not easy to get a fishing booking in the Loch Maree Hotel.

I succeeded in 1950. We had been comfortable at Kinlochewe and I was sorry to be leaving Alister Matthieson, but I could not resist the chance of the wonderful fishing at Loch Maree. Arriving at the hotel in the fishing season was reminiscent of the arrival of a new boy at a public school. At the hotel the prefects were in the shape of experienced anglers, ruling the roost, enjoying the services of the best ghillies with the best boats. Newcomers were allocated a leaky old boat with a defective outboard engine, and one of the weaker links in the team of ghillies. At night, the newcomer was seized upon by fishing bores; one-track-mind men, always ready to pounce on the new boy and pour out their words of wisdom on fishing practice.

Staying at Loch Maree for over twenty years has convinced me that there is something about fishing that can be bad for the character. It is a fever, the symptoms of which are an overwhelming desire to catch fish, a passionate drive to excel, with a danger of becoming pettily dishonest: yet of all pastimes there is nothing more absorbing. It requires patience, concentration, painfully acquired skill and indomitable tenacity of purpose. It is no wonder that when a fisherman eventually succeeds in becoming reasonably skilful he is in danger of becoming boring and boastful.

The management at the Loch Maree Hotel was similar to the management at Kinlochewe Lodge, inefficient and unskilled. In my second year there, there was a change of management. The wife of the new manager was an excellent cook, but the manager was making heavy weather of things. He told me that the hotel was not paying its way and that he thought the syndicate that owned the company was wanting to sell. He also told me that in his management agreement there was a clause giving him the first option to purchase in case the hotel should be sold.

Whilst we were staying in the hotel in 1953 the matter came to a head and the hotel company was put on the market. The manager had no money to exercise his option, but he agreed that I should go with him to Inverness to discuss the matter with the company's solicitors. When we returned, I had negotiated the purchase and paid the deposit. The return from Inverness was a protracted business; the manager seemed to be friendly with every licensed hotel-keeper on our route, and by the time we arrived back at Loch Maree he was in a very elevated condition.

The hotel was full of anglers, and from them a syndicate of twelve was formed to take up the purchase — all old customers with the exception of myself. From the start it was agreed by all the subscribers that it was not to be looked upon as an investment requiring a normal commercial return, but as having the primary object of preserving and improving the fishing amenities of the Loch Maree Hotel.

The syndicate met at Perth in the autumn. The original policy was affirmed, a board of four directors — all Scotsmen with the exception of myself — was appointed to carry it out. Being the only director with any experience of the hotel business I was made chairman and had to take the major part of the responsibility. By taking the initiative in buying the company, I had destroyed my holiday peace.

The first action of the board was to adopt a new set of angling rules under which all the fishing guests enjoyed the same facilities. Jockeying for the best boats was made impossible; newcomers were put on level terms with the habitués. A fleet of new boats was ordered from Mac-Donald, the Highland boat builder whose workshop was at Alligin on the shore of Loch Torridon, and these were equipped with new outboard motors. A jetty was built, and in course of time an excellent rod house nearby. The improved fishing conditions attracted and held a team of experienced ghillies, and the over-all result was a rapid improvement in the general fishing conditions.

The responsibility for the direction of the hotel mostly fell on me, and there were plenty of difficulties. The manager at the time of the purchase only lasted two years. The next appointment made was a young married Scotsman, a colourful character who wore the kilt, who made a good impression. But, at the end of the season, his management showed a substantial loss.

The next appointment made was a manageress — Miss Alexander. She was very experienced in the hotel business, well trained, with high standards, and a formidable character. It was a relief to me to be dealing with a fellow hotel-keeper, but not all the customers appreciated the staider atmosphere that accompanied the more comfortable conditions. The management of Miss Alexander quickly pulled the hotel round and turned the loss into a profit. She was a nice-looking, sturdily built woman, reserved, responsive to courtesy and (we were to find out) even more responsive to aggression and rudeness.

There was a disaster during her first season. She over-booked the fishing at a vital time of the year. The error was discovered at the start of the sea trout season, which sets off with a bang when the sea trout run in from the

sea at the beginning of July. Anglers arrived at the hotel
to find that two more boats had been booked than could
be provided. There was a near riot; I was not there at the
time but I was told that the situation was tense. The
anglers held a meeting in the lounge, tempers rose, bad
language was used and Miss Alexander was made the scape-
goat by the furious fishermen. She had not bowed to the
storm; the bad behaviour of some of the thwarted anglers
had roused her and she had reacted indignantly to their
rudeness.

At the time the storm broke I was thirty miles further
north, fishing the Gruinard river as the guest of a friend,
Rob Ferens. Another friend of mine staying at Loch Maree
rang up to tell me of the maelstrom in the hotel. I was due
to arrive there the following Sunday. "When you arrive",
he said, "they will skin you alive!". I had caught five
salmon that day, so I was feeling fit to cope with any
emergency.

When I arrived at the hotel the situation was indeed
tense, as there was still one boat overbooked for the
following two weeks. I put the matter straight by giving
up our boat for as long as the shortage remained. This was
not too well received – the indignant anglers felt that they
had been robbed of a juicy grievance! However the situation was solved in an unforeseen manner. One of the
anglers had a heart attack on the Sunday evening of our
arrival, and he and his companion left the hotel by ambu-
lance. The overbooking was solved.

The consequences of the row lasted a long time. Some
of the anglers took a permanent dislike to Miss Alexander
and nothing she did could please them. She was too
firm a character to attempt to ingratiate herself with her
critics, and for a period of years there were two factions
in the hotel, one for Miss Alexander and one against. I
was for her; I knew that she had pulled the hotel round,
and I appreciated her ability in coping with the difficulties

of running an hotel in such a remote area. So I did every-thing I could to support her.

The affair had a strange climax. One of Miss Alexander's principal supporters in the syndicate was a Captain Donald, an elderly solicitor from Dundee and an ex-Gordon Highlander, who spent two months every year at Loch Maree and who had become a patriarchal figure in the hotel. When I first knew him he was approaching ninety years of age. When eventually he died, his funeral at Dundee was attended by all the Scottish members of the syndicate. After the funeral they put their heads together and decided that Miss Alexander must go; also that as I supported her I should be replaced as chairman. A special meeting of the full syndicate was called. One of the plotters was unwise enough to tell me what was in the wind. I knew four members of the syndicate who would support me. Two of the original members had died, so to strengthen my position I bought their shares.

The meeting was held in Edinburgh. I arrived and was confronted by the five Scotsmen. There were only six of us at the meeting — the five Scotsmen and myself. As chairman I started the meeting by giving a brief statement as to why I supported Miss Alexander. I was followed by two or three members who thanked me for my services, rebuked me for my obstinacy, and informed me that they had decided that I must be replaced. The motion for my removal was proposed and seconded. I put it to the meet-ing and at the same time I produced four proxies plus my own triple holding, so the motion was defeated. The five Scotsmen were in a state of shock; one of them expressed himself so forcibly that I warned him of the danger of a thrombosis; it was unfortunate, as apparently he had had one only a short time before. At the break up of the meeting one of the members refused to shake my hand.

The following autumn, I called another special meeting and tendered my resignation, explaining that I would not be a party to the dismissal of Miss Alexander, but that I did not want to force my views on the other members of the syndicate. By this time tempers had cooled. It had been ascertained that Miss Alexander was approaching the age of retirement, and therefore there was no further need for controversy. I was asked to stay on as chairman, and as the request was unanimous I consented. The following year Miss Alexander retired with flying colours.

After their experience of battling with a determined Scotswoman, the members told me the general feeling was that the next manager should be a man. The post was advertised, and we received over one hundred and twenty applications, including an extremely good one from a Miss Kathleen Moodie. Miss Moodie was appointed; she has been a success, and today the hotel is as good as ever.

Esmé and I never allowed these ups and downs to interfere with the pleasure of our holiday. In the hotel we were very comfortably fixed, having the bedroom and sitting room that Queen Victoria occupied in 1874 when she stayed at the Loch Maree Hotel for the best part of a week.

On the loch we were looked after by Donald Urquhart, the ghillie I had met at Kinlochewe. He was a true Western Highlander; his native tongue was the Gaelic, which he spoke more readily than he spoke English. He was a stone-mason by trade, but his life centred round the struggle to grow crops and raise stock on the poor peaty land of his croft on the shore of the Gairloch. He had a wild quality, a natural dignity and a philosophical outlook. His often repeated saying — "Enough is enough" — was a true expression of his attitude to life. Except in one respect, we could never catch enough sea trout to satisfy him. He loved Esmé and always treated her with the greatest courtesy and consideration. When she was in the boat, the one thing he wanted to do was to please her. "What does the lady want to do?" he would say. Esmé, who was quite happy anyway, and who regarded fishing as rather a sick joke, would make some suggestion to keep Donald happy. If I disagreed he would turn to me and say, "You, you're an awful man". Then he would do as Esmé had suggested.

I have heard it said that golf is the game with the largest percentage of possible errors, but I think that dapping for sea trout could run it pretty close. In dapping, an artificial fly on the end of a blow line is floated on the surface of the water so that it flits along like a low-flying moth. When a fish is attracted, it may take the fly greedily or miss it; or it may suck it down slowly; sometimes it will roll on it, to drown it, and take it below the surface. The angler's eye must never leave the fly, so that if a fish does rise he can react in the appropriate way to hook it.

One of the ghillies, who must be nameless, distilled whisky up the hill in the region of his croft. It was never sold, but was one of his contributions to the life of his district. Sometimes, I was privileged to be given a bottle of this colourless, extremely strong, and very comforting brew. It had to be sipped, and as it went down it generated a warming glow in the stomach. One day, a bottle of colourless liquid arrived by parcel post at the Royal. Not realising what it was, I stood it on the top of a steel filing cabinet in my office. My brother called and I drew his attention to the mysterious bottle. Frank inspected it closely in its virgin purity — just a bottle of pure clear liquid — "I wonder if it is a bottle of Holy Water", he mused. As he pronounced the words "Holy Water" the cork blew off. Then I knew in a flash what it contained!

CHAPTER XIX

MOSTLY ABOUT ART COLLECTING

Back at home, the strength of the business was growing. After the first few post-war years the bulk of the holiday accommodation for the summer season was booked from one year to the next, and at the bank holiday weekends the hotel could have been booked five times over.

The conference business was also growing. The Royal had been the first hotel in the north of England to cater specifically for the conference business. The demand had grown so steadily that after the third post-war year we were able to keep the hotel open all the year round, and to employ all our important staff on a permanent basis.

The conference business had all sorts of special requirements. One was a need for a number of private suites, so the whole of the first floor was converted into this type of accommodation. We named the suite next to the "Winston Churchill" suite the "Sitwell suite", in recognition of the connection of the Sitwell family with Scarborough and their connections with our hotels. When Osbert Sitwell heard about the new suite, he telephoned from his country house in Derbyshire to say that he was bringing his sister Edith to see it. He reserved a table for lunch. He arrived, looking very patrician, carrying a silver-topped ebony cane. Edith looked even more distinguished — she had a medieval quality. Meeting them again reminded me of the days when their parents stayed with us at the Pavilion; they, too, were distinguished, but not, I thought, quite as unique as Osbert and Edith. When I took them up to the suite, Edith went to the sitting room window to look at the familiar view over the old town with the harbour nestling at the foot, whilst Osbert looked around the room with close attention. It had distinction and a certain special character. Both John Hill and I had had the Sitwells in mind when it was designed. Amongst other things, there was a small painting by John Armstrong of a monastery above Amalfi which took Osbert's fancy. At length, he drew himself up and looking me straight in the eye said: "Mr. Laughton, I can only tell you that we are highly honoured".

I asked Osbert whether I might order the wine for his lunch. He agreed. In the cellars, we had a delicious "Wehlener Sonnenuhr" and I ordered a bottle to be brought straight from the cellar as they entered the restaurant. Towards the end of the meal, I went to their table to ask if they had enjoyed their lunch, especially the wine. "Won't you join us in a glass?", Osbert said, and he ordered another bottle. It really was delicious; it confirmed my view that fine Moselle is the best of all luncheon wines. After the meal, Osbert was surprised to find that the wine was not on his bill and when he said goodbye he remarked on this. I told him that I had his permission to deal with the wine. "To think", he replied in mock horror, "that I had the audacity to order another bottle".

He was impressed by the hotel and subsequently stayed with us several times. On one occasion he brought Edith with him for an extended visit. One of the attractions for him was the picture collection, which was constantly growing. After their visit I received a letter from Edith. She wrote: "I am more impressed than it would be possible to say, at the work you are doing, in making the public see Art as something to be enjoyed as a holiday delight. It really is most extraordinary. There is no doubt at all that you are a pioneer in this way, and I am sure that you will be the means of bringing quite a new happiness into many lives".

I had found John Martin's twenty-four oil sketches —
the preliminary studies for his twenty-four famous
engravings for "Paradise Lost". They were dark in tone
but I hung them together illuminated by picture lights,
which brought them to life. I also found a beautiful small
oil painting of Whitby by John Martin, and I hung this in
the Sitwell sitting room. Osbert saw it and was enchanted.

When Kenneth Clark stayed at the hotel, he occupied
the Sitwell suite. His favourite in the collection seemed
to be a large painting by John Martin of "Sodom and
Gomorrah", which hung on the Wellington staircase
in company with a magnificent landscape by John Dun-
thorne (who was Constable's painting assistant), a large
painting by William Etty of "The Judgement of Paris"
and other fine things.

Walking round the hotel was like visiting a series of
small exhibitions, each with its own special character. On
the first floor there was a collection of the works of an
enchanting painter, G. W. Mote. Nobody seemed to have
heard of him. He lived to a good age, born in 1832 he
died in 1909. His middle period was superb. I commissioned a dealer, Robert Frank, who specialised in works
of the English nineteenth century painters, to search for
his work. I succeeded in acquiring a group that hung
together beautifully on the first floor.

On the floor above, I hung the John Martins' and on
the floor above that a collection of paintings of poultry
and animals by William Huggins. They were of such
quality that I could not understand why I was able to
acquire them for such reasonable prices.

One of the rarest things I bought was a fascinating
painting of Jerusalem, depicted as a medieval walled town
with beautiful, early Gothic buildings. In the left-hand
foreground is the dead Christ; at the foot of the cross and
in the right-hand foreground are the three Mary's. It was
hanging in the antique department of a store in Hull — the

price thirty pounds. An expert visiting the hotel told me it was a painting by Monsu Desiderio. Later still an American dealer arrived at the hotel for the specific purpose of buying it. He offered me six thousand pounds but I refused. He would have offered more, but I told him it was useless. I had bought it at a price I could afford and I intended to keep it.

John Rickett, who was then the head of the picture department in Sotheby's, heard about the collection and visited the hotel. He was astonished by the quality of the pictures and offered to go round the collection with the catalogue and pencil in the values. When he gave me back the catalogue I was incredulous of the values that he had pencilled in. To convince me he persuaded me to send to the saleroom thirty small paintings to test his valuation. He said, "You have so many, you will never miss them". The sale more than proved his judgement. The thirty paintings fetched thirty-two thousand pounds; they had cost two thousand two hundred. I have never ceased to regret the sale — they were irreplaceable. The truth is, I am a collector not a dealer.

There was another side to my collecting. I felt that I should also collect contemporary work, but this presented a far greater challenge. I had found it difficult to understand and appreciate the work of the nineteenth century European masters. It was still more difficult to weigh up and select from the work of my own generation. I bought several works by R. O. Dunlop, a Victor Pasmore, a Graham Sutherland, two Matthew Smiths and five Ivon Hitchens. I also bought from the artists who had worked with me in the hotels: Bruce Turner, Edward Bawden, Eric Ravilious and John Armstrong. In 1951 I came across the work of Ruszkowski.

The paintings of Ruszkowski made a strong impression upon me, so much so that my interest in contemporary painting concentrated on his work. He had an exhibition at the Roland, Browse and Delbanco gallery in 1952, from which I bought two paintings; they were the only paintings sold during a month's exhibition. Dr. Roland told me where I could get in touch with him, so I sought him out. Ruszkowski was a Pole. He had come to this country in the course of his war service, married an English woman and settled here. I met him on the steps of the Hampstead School of Art. He was a medium-sized man, trim, with deep piercing eyes. We had a stilted meeting, at which he said little. I told him how much I was struck by his work and that, although I was only an unimportant collector, I was convinced that he was an important artist.

It was at a time when he was discouraged by his lack of success. Years later he told me that when we met, his situation was so bad that he was thinking that he would have to give up his painting and turn to something else to earn a living. My interest encouraged him to struggle on. We became friends, almost collaborators. I collected his work and did what I could to further his interests, over a period of twenty years. He became my mentor in art as Bruce Turner had been in my early collecting days.

In 1959 I took him to Loch Maree for a short visit. We spent our days in a boat on the loch. Passing between the islands he kept repeating, "This is paradise". In the evening, after dinner, we would stroll together through the woodland on the hillside sloping up from the hotel. One evening we came across a deserted small farm, with a range of old stone buildings and with a small galvanised metal shack at one end. Peering through the shack window he turned to me and said, "I could live here and paint". I looked in at a filthy jumble of rubbish, including an old iron bedstead. "But where would you sleep?", I asked. "In there", he replied, "there is a bed". We looked round the deserted buildings to see if there was a room suitable for a studio. He picked on the hay-loft, but the hay-door was missing. "If there was glass in that", he said, "it would make a studio".

I was able to obtain permission for him to live in the galvanised shack and to use the hay-loft as his studio. A glass door was installed, and the rotting floor of the loft partially renewed. The following year, he took his canvases to Loch Maree and painted there for over three months.

I motored up to see how he was getting on, to find him living a spartan life, neglecting everything save his painting. After dinner together at the hotel, we adjourned to his shack, where he put a lighted candle into a bottle neck and we talked until the early hours.

He returned to Loch Maree the following year, this time taking with him his newly acquired dog, Kita. She provided company for him and reminded him of the necessity for regular food. I motored up again and this time he took me to a dark rocky ravine, where he had found subjects for his painting. The outcome of his two visits was a number of magnificent works, some of which I acquired.

His paintings gradually took over the wall space of the modern section of the collection. I sometimes wondered whether the customers would find them difficult and even possibly resent them. However, the collection in the hotel was so widespread in its range that some section of it was bound to interest and please almost everybody. In my collecting I usually had at the back of my mind the wish to give our customers pleasure. But in the case of Ruszkowski the dominant thought was my own interest and appreciation.

CHAPTER XX

A MIXED BAG

In 1953, Sir Brian Robertson, the chairman of British Railways, offered me a seat on the Railway Hotel and Catering Sub-commission which was in effect the board of directors controlling all the railway hotels and all the railway catering. My friend Harry Methven, now Sir Harry, was the chairman, so I accepted. I was astonished to find that there were only four members and that apart from myself none of them were hotel-keepers. I found that the board was entirely in the hands of the permanent officials led by a very able general manager, Frank Hole. We were cosseted, given luxurious accommodation, gargantuan lunches and unlimited supplies of liquor. In return we were expected to endorse and approve the work of the permanent officials presented to us in the form of well drawn up accounts. I am not a "figure man" and as all our decisions were based on the figures before us, I felt compelled to get to closer quarters with the problems with which we had to deal. During the first year of my appointment I spent as much time as I could spare visiting the hotels. This gave me the opportunity to study the restaurant cars and refreshment rooms as I travelled round the country. In the course of my investigations I had some fascinating experiences.

I had noted, at the Caledonian Hotel, Edinburgh, that the smoked salmon was exceptionally good. Later, talking to the chef in his kitchens, I asked him where his smoked salmon came from and he told me that he smoked it himself. I asked him diffidently if he would tell me his method. "Certainly", he said, "I would tell you anything.

You are the only director who has ever visited my kitchens".
His recipe included the use of juniper twigs, so when I
arrived back at home I planted four juniper trees. Eventually I built myself a small smoking plant based on his
instructions which still produces delicious smoked fish.

I made it a practice to visit all departments in every
hotel, establishing a friendly relationship with staff of
every grade. My methods seemed to cause uneasiness
amongst the head office administrative staff, but they
gradually came to accept them. In course of time I established a close rapport with Frank Hole, who made more
and more use of my services. After I had served several
years, I began to realize that Sir Brian Robertson was
interested in what I was doing. The time for Sir Harry
Methven's retirement was approaching and it seemed as
though he was thinking of me as a possible successor. It
was interesting, but I knew that to be an effective chairman I should need a change of conditions. It would
have been impossible for me to have any real effect serving
on a part-time basis. It would have needed a sustained
concentrated effort to have achieved the policy I had in
mind. I thought that on the hotel side a policy of expansion was required and that the restaurant cars and the
refreshment rooms needed to be re-organised. I discussed
the possibilities with Esmé. When I told her that it might
mean leaving Scarborough and living in London, she was
against it. She could not see the sense in abandoning our
own business, in which we had the freedom to follow our
own inclinations, to work for a nationalised organisation.

One day I had word from Sir Brian asking me to meet
him at Leeds and indicating that he had something important to discuss. Both Esmé and I sensed that the time for
decision had come. I was attracted by the idea of heading
such a large hotel organisation, but I felt instinctively that
Esmé's attitude was sensible and right. I promised her
I would not make any arrangements that meant we should

have to leave our home in Scarborough.

I found Sir Brian at the Queen's Hotel, Leeds, surrounded by staff. He drew me aside and told me that he wished me to travel with him to York in his special train in which we would be able to have a private discussion. When we were alone together in the office of his saloon carriage he told me that he proposed to appoint me to the North-Eastern Railway Management Board as a step towards my becoming a part-time Transport Commissioner which would qualify me to act as chairman of the Hotel and Catering Sub-commission. He was thinking of a part-time chairmanship but I knew that only a full-time appointment could be really effective. I declined his offer partly because I knew that we were at cross purposes, but principally because of my promise to Esmé. Sir Brian's reaction was one of disgusted astonishment, one of the phrases he used has stayed in my memory. "It's an honour, you know", he said looking at me with incredulous distaste. It finished me with him — he never spoke to me again.

When Dr. Beeching succeeded Sir Brian as chairman, the Hotel and Catering Sub-commission was reconstituted and I was dropped. I had been on the board nine years. I had found it interesting and sometimes enjoyable but the trouble was that most of the time it was frustrating and ineffective. It had not interfered much with my work at home. Certainly, the things I learned had more than compensated for the time I had spent.

Mother died in 1955. She was the creator of our family fortune — even before the death of father in 1924 she had taken the lead. She was scarred by the experiences of her girlhood, when her father had been made bankrupt, and she had seen him transformed from a generous and popular innkeeper into an unwanted has-been. Mother knew from experience how transient and self-interested customers' favour can be. She had earned the respect and affection of the Pavilion customers, but she never traded on it.

She prided herself on not accepting hospitality, and she told us many times that she had never had a meal of any sort in a private house in Scarborough. In the hotel, no customer would have presumed to ask her to have a drink. In her own field she was a *grande dame*, one of the few women who became a legend in her own lifetime.

She had brought up three families: her own three boys, and also Stewart and Jack Dewsbury and Mollie and Letitia Nasbet, the children of her two younger sisters, both of whom had died whilst their children were still young. It was Stewart and Jack's father who financed our move to the Pavilion.

Mother retained her faculties until the last, and when she died she left behind a family of seven – all equally impressed by her sterling qualities. Towards her end, she discussed the future of the Pavilion with Frank. She knew he was delicate and advised him to sell, for she knew that he found running the hotel a strain.

On mother's death the staff at the Pavilion transferred their loyalty to Frank. They were an exceptional group – not only the staff at the front of the house, but also those behind the scenes. Under Frank's direction they made the Pavilion the best hotel in the north of England.

It was sad that it had to be sold – had Frank been more robust he would have carried on. In selling, one of his main considerations was the interests of the staff. In the early 1960's he refused a bid of thirty thousand pounds – more than he actually sold for – because the bidders were intending to knock down the hotel to re-develop the site. Eventually he sold to a property company with a local chairman and was given an undertaking that the Pavilion would be run as an hotel for at least ten years. When Frank sold the property, it was understood that all the staff would be retained – some of them were still there in 1971 when the new owners closed the hotel.

After Frank retired from the Pavilion I decided to open

a small *à la carte* restaurant, with less than thirty covers and having its own kitchen which I named "The Gourmet". When I told Frank about it he looked doubtful and said, "That's a name that will take a bit of living up to". It was enjoyable setting it up, and it proved to be a great asset to the Royal.

Frank moved from the Pavilion to his home in Scalby outside Scarborough. He was planning to live in the South of France. He had a holiday villa at Biot, in the hills above Antibes, but it was large for his purpose. So he sold it and bought an apartment in Antibes and that was where he was planning to retire to.

In the early summer of 1955 we had an interesting guest at the Royal Hotel, Hermione Gingold. Her son, Stephen Joseph, was a young university lecturer, head of the drama department of Manchester University. Stephen had come to Scarborough to run a season of plays in the Concert Room at the Scarborough Public Library. He had adopted the American "Theatre-in-the-Round" plan. The opening of his theatre was to be in June. He called to see me to enlist my support and he asked whether the hotel would entertain his mother for the opening night. She arrived a rather bizarre-looking dowager, I took her up to a private suite and she immediately expressed her doubts. "Stephen is a strange boy", she said, "I hope he knows what he's about". After the performance she was reassured. I gave a small party for her in my office, she was in splendid form and gave her magnificent rendering of a formidable female determined to be as outrageous as possible. Esmé, Stephen and I made a small but appreciative audience.

The first season was a great struggle for Stephen. The box office receipts were not sufficient to cover the actors' salaries, so Stephen made up the deficiency by taking a part-time job as a coal heaver. The second season was the same but this season he worked as a part-time brewer's drayman. One of the reasons for his lack of commercial success was his determination to provide a forum for young dramatists. The third season, he engaged a young man as an assistant stage manager, Alan Ayckbourn. Stephen spotted that he had talent and suggested that he should try his hand at playwriting. He commissioned him to write a play for the following season, which after much pressing he did. It was largely due to Stephen that Alan was launched as a playwright. Practically every one of his brilliant comedies has been written for the Scarborough Theatre-in-the-Round.

Stephen settled in Scarborough where he bought a beautiful house in the old town overlooking the harbour, and founded "The Scarborough Theatre Trust". Every year his theatre gathered strength. Unfortunately he fell seriously ill in the course of his last season in 1965, and died in 1967. His work was taken over by Alan Ayckbourn, who became theatre director and resident playwright. I was a member of the Theatre Council and eventually became chairman. Over the nineteen years that the theatre has been established, I have seen it fulfil the original conception of its founder, Stephen Joseph. Now it provides a forum and workshop for a widespread group of authors and Alan himself has developed into the most successful playwright of his generation. Today our theatre is one of the sources of modern comedy, with a group of authors, a brilliant group of players, creative direction and an ever-growing audience.

My connection with the theatre fitted in with my work in the hotel. With the sale of the Pavilion, and my release from the Railway Hotel and Catering Board, I had plenty of time. The Royal was running smoothly except in the conference period, during which it had to be transformed to meet the multifarious requirements of the conference organisers. These could be astonishing. We accommodated sales conferences, local government conferences,

Trade Union conferences, trade associations, and medical conferences; the most fascinating of all were the political conferences. During political conferences, the hotel became for a brief few days a centre of public attention, with a television studio in one section of the building, and a radio studio in another. On one occasion, a live television programme was going out when the producers found themselves short of an item. One of the producers seized hold of me and rushed me down to be interviewed by Robin Day. It was no good talking to me about politics, so he decided to discuss the hotel, asking me about the collection of pictures. During the interview he mentioned that there was an attractive painting in his room but no telephone. He then shot at me, "Mr. Laughton, do you consider a painting more important than a telephone?" It was not an easy one, "I do", I replied, "but in this case it's the fault of the G.P.O., the telephones are all on order. Yours is one of the very few rooms left without one".

The political conference I remember best was the Labour Conference of 1960, when Hugh Gaitskell was the leader of the party in opposition. At the start of the conference it was universally considered that Gaitskell was a falling star. The press and the broadcasters were all saying that it was going to be his last appearance as leader of the party. It was a strange situation; Gaitskell was the leader, but in the hotel one noticed that he was an isolated figure. He and his wife had a table to themselves in the restaurant; nobody seemed to bother about them. Other well-known figures seemed to be the centre of attention. I was told more than once that Gaitskell was finished. It was a matter of regret to me, as there was an unusual aura of strength and repose about him that impressed me.

The climax of the conference was to be the final meeting, at which he was to be the principal speaker, and it was to take place in the afternoon at the Spa Grand Hall. That morning Gaitskell told me that he would like to lunch in his private sitting room. As lunch was progressing, I slipped up to his suite to make certain that he was being served. I put my head round the door — lunch was there, but Gaitskell was at his desk writing frantically. He was composing his speech for that afternoon.

One of the leading delegates offered me a seat on the platform, so I went to the meeting. The conference hall was agog — it is not often that one participates in the fall of a leader. Gaitskell rose to speak. Up to then, the best political speech I had heard had been given by Aneurin Bevan, but it did not equal this speech. Gaitskell challenged the whole meeting. "What do you take me for?" he asked. He refused to give ground, and in his final passage he told them, "I will fight and fight and fight again". He sat down to a stunned silence that suddenly erupted into frantic cheering — cheering from almost everyone except the platform. Those on the front row of the platform were sitting silent, in dazed amazement. Gaitskell was still the leader, and he remained the leader until his premature death. The next time the leaders of the Labour party stayed at the Royal, Mr. Wilson was leading them as Prime Minister.

On one of his visits as Prime Minister he asked for me as he was leaving. I joined him at the entrance to the hotel. "I wanted to see you before I left", he said, "to tell you that we all think this is the best hotel that we visit, and further not only do we politicians think so, but so also do the pressmen". It was clear that he thought that if we could get by with the press, then we really must be good!

CHAPTER XXI

DEATH OF CHARLES

In the autumn of 1961 we had news from Elsa that Charles was desperately ill. Neither Frank nor I had seen much of him since the war. He had played a season at Stratford-on-Avon in 1959, where I went to see him play Lear, but he was not in good health. Years before he had reduced me to tears reading Lear in our bedroom at Monsieur Dumaine's hotel at Saulieu. I wish he had played Lear in his prime, for in 1959 the shadow of the illness that was coming was affecting him.

As soon as I heard from Elsa that Charles was in the Cedars of Lebanon Hospital, Los Angeles, I dropped everything and flew over. It was a shock to see him. He had lost a tremendous lot of flesh, but even so his head looked magnificent. He was suffering a great deal of pain and had got to the stage when drugs could not give him complete relief. It was wonderful to be with him again; we had so much to talk about; but one subject to the forefront of my mind was difficult to broach. The intensive propaganda of the Jesuits had turned Charles against religion and I knew that not long after leaving Stonyhurst he had ceased to practise. He had not the benefit of the simple teaching of Father Cassidy at the preparatory school, Hodder Place, as I had.

I could not bear the thought of Charles lying there, knowing he was dying and with no faith. One day he said to me, "I suppose you still go to church?" "Yes", I said. "Where do you go here?" he asked. I told him that I had first gone to a church run by the Jesuits in the Sunset Boulevard, but that it was too efficient and I had not felt at home there. At the end of the Mass somebody switched on a fan which set an American flag fluttering above the corner of the altar. I had left with a feeling of nausea. After that I found a church nearer to Charles' home, in which the parish priest was an elderly Italian; after Mass I had a talk with him in the sacristy. The priest was a simple old man whom I thought would have suited Charles. He reminded me of Father Pantalleoni, a priest at Ravello, near Amalfi, who had become a friend of Charles and Elsa. Father Pantelleoni had built a shrine to Our Lady with a spring nearby, which he asserted was Aqua Miraculoso. His church was decked with discarded crutches, the evidence of many miraculous cures. Father Pantalleone's gaiety and simple faith had appealed to both Elsa and Charles. I got the old Italian priest from the nearby church to promise to go himself to attend to Charles if ever there was a call, as I thought he too was a man whom Charles would appreciate.

I was having a difficult time with Elsa. We had never got on well together — we were so different. Elsa had a keen critical mind, whilst I am inclined towards uncritical appreciation. Mockery was the speciality of Elsa's work; anything depending on faith rather than experience was foreign to her. It was not surprising, therefore, that she despised religion. She knew my concern for Charles' lack of faith. Her attitude was that it would be despicable for him to see a priest at a time when he knew that he was dying. She told me that in her eyes the bravest thing that Charles had ever done was during the first world war when he had refused the ministrations of a priest before going over the top to attack the German lines. It was useless for me to try to explain my feelings to her; she hated the Catholic church and she was determined that Charles should have nothing to do with it.

She had given instructions that if a priest called he should not be allowed to see him at the hospital, and she indicated to me that I was wasting my time. During my visit she was constantly railing at the deficiences of the Catholic church in America. To Elsa, homosexuality was a term of abuse, and she seemed to imagine that the church was riddled with it from the parish priests up to the Cardinals.

Charles had three nurses — two of them Catholics, the third a young Australian girl. They were all aware of Elsa's attitude. To my surprise the young Australian nurse, who was not a Catholic, broached the subject; "I know what you are feeling about Charles", she said, "I shall do anything I can to help you".

There was very little I could do. I had no intention of asking a priest to go to see Charles; all I wanted was that if Charles himself asked to see a priest, a priest should be allowed to see him. If this did happen, I wanted him to be a simple man who would be likely to appeal to him but whilst I was there the situation did not arise.

Charles' and Elsa's home was not far from the hospital. It was an old fashioned Edwardian house on the lower slopes of the hills above Hollywood. It was full of paintings, hundreds of books, and pre-Columbian sculpture all collected by Charles. Charles had a work-room in which there were three De Stael paintings. The best feature of the house was the swimming pool — designed by Lloyd Wright junior — which could be approached from a staircase leading directly out of my bedroom. If I had been more at home with Elsa, I should have appreciated better the delightful surroundings. As the situation stood, it was a relief to escape to Charles at the hospital. We were happy to be together again, reminiscing about our early days at home, the farm at Lockton, and his struggles to establish himself in the theatre. Very little was said about religion. Charles knew that I held to my faith and that I wanted to help him to regain his. I was able to tell him that I knew he had done his best with his talents, and for that reason alone I was certain that he would be rewarded — that is as far as I got.

At times, his pain broke through the drugs, and these times were becoming more frequent. At length, the time came for Frank to arrive from England to replace me. I was to leave one evening and Frank was due to arrive the following morning. I stayed with Charles until the last possible moment before catching the plane. It was dreadful leaving him; he meant so much to me. I can never express how much he has enriched my life.

Frank, who was a very good nurse, arrived the following day. I am sure that in Charles' last stages he was more use than I could have been. I left a note for Frank telling him about the old Italian priest. Not long after I left, Frank was with Charles when he was in great pain. He called out, "Can't you help me?" There was nothing Frank could do. "I can't, Charles", he said, "would you like to see a priest?" "Yes", said Charles. Frank fetched the old Italian priest and after his first visit he saw him every day up to the day of his death. Soon after this, Charles was taken home, as nothing more could be done for him at the hospital, and before he died he was received back into the church.

Charles had had a hard life. He had been very successful but it had been at a great cost. The little I had seen of the film world in his Mayflower days had made me realise what a jungle it was. I had seen very little of him since he went to the States, but on the occasions I did see him I was not reassured. The happiest days of his life were his early days in the theatre, the days when he and Elsa had a house in the country, tucked away in the Surrey woodlands, and their home in Gordon Square. I think his life would have been happier had he stayed in England and concentrated on the stage. He would have been more his own master, mixing with people of his own kind, and with a better chance of living a satisfying, creative life.

There would have been no Captain Bligh and no Senator Cooley, that wonderfully prophetic performance in the film *Advise and Consent*. They were the highlights of the years spent on the Hollywood treadmill. Towards the end of his life he found a further outlet for his energies; he became a story-teller, travelling thousands of miles all over the United States reading to many thousands of people.

He became a much loved figure, partly due to his direct contact with the American public in the course of his reading tours. He was something more than an actor; he was a teacher. The cinema had taken him further and further away from his audience; it had made him a rich man but not a happy one. His readings brought the audiences back to him, renewing his satisfaction in his work and making him a happier and a more fulfilled man.

Of all his films the one that gave me the most pleasure was *Rembrandt,* made in 1936 — a beautiful film which set out to portray the struggle of the creative artist to remain true to his genius. The film was written by Carl Zuckmayer, produced and directed by Alexander Korda and designed by his brother, Vincent Korda. Charles was supported by a fine team of English actors and actresses, amongst whom Elsa Lanchester stood out. Her portrayal of Hendrickje Stoffels was beautiful, touching and convincing. Never have I seen a better husband and wife performance.

CHAPTER XXII

DEATH OF FRANK

When Frank returned from Holywood, he started to prepare for his move to France. He sold his house in Scalby and moved to a flat in London. He was planning to go to his apartment in Antibes in the spring of 1964.

Nineteen sixty-three was a very busy year in the hotel. The Gourmet Restaurant was a success and it added a new dimension to the Royal. I had found an exceptionally good *à la carte* chef, Reno Santini, and I promoted Ken Matthews, the best of our young apprentice chefs, to be his commis; as I already had a particularly fine patissier, Chef Colin Quinn, the *carte* was exceptional in quality. The team of chefs combined with the resources of the extensive cellar, produced a really good restaurant.

We were beginning to find the conferences very hard going. The late night functions were liable to leave the hotel in a shocking mess, and it was extremely difficult for the night staff to clean up by morning. Esmé became so disturbed that she began to work right through the night to help to get the hotel into shape. I would have liked to stop her doing so, but she could not stand seeing the place deteriorate. By the end of the autumn conference season we were both exhausted.

Just after Christmas, I had a telephone call from London. Frank, who had been having severe headaches had been taken to the Hospital for Nervous Diseases in Queen's Square, following a stroke. When I arrived at the hospital he seemed to have recovered partially, and he was well enough to undergo some form of cerebral examination.

I managed to get a room in an hotel close by, and I got back to the hospital just before his examination was finished. After he returned to the ward, the registrar drew me aside. It was bad news; he had a tumour in the brain which was probably malignant. He was to be moved to a surgical ward, and would be operated on in a few days' time.

I remained in London and I was allowed to visit him whenever I liked. I went with him from the general ward on the ground floor to the surgical ward on an upper floor. He was in a wheel chair and desperately ill, but he still had his dry sense of humour. When we got to the lift, as the button was pressed to take us up he said, "I'm glad we are going up". "Why?", I asked. "Down leads to the mortuary", he replied.

A few days later he was being prepared for the operation. A label on a rubber band was put on his wrist. He regarded it quizzically and said, "That's to see that the corpses don't get mixed". The operating theatre was on the floor above the ward and I went with him as far as the lift. When I returned later I found him back in the same ward — he had not been operated upon. The patient before him had died on the operating table, and the surgeon had ceased operating for the day. Frank was stoical and cheerful, but with a sense of premonition. After a few days the operation took place; the tumour proved to be large and malignant — nothing could be done. He lingered on for five weeks, unconscious practically all the time. Just once he became fully conscious; he asked for a cup of coffee, and, as an afterthought, a brandy. I was rushing out to buy the brandy when the Sister stopped me. "We have it, we will serve it with the coffee", she said. He was himself for almost half an hour, but they were his last fully conscious moments.

I rang Hollywood to tell Elsa, as she was very fond of Frank. She flew over immediately and was distressed to find him unconscious. She surprised me by asking, "Has he got a good priest?" Frank had succeeded where I had failed in making Elsa realise that there are circumstances when priests have their uses.

Frank was in a surgical ward with four beds. Although he was unconscious, I felt he sensed my presence and sometimes when I spoke to him I thought I could feel a responsive pressure from his hand. One day, a distressed patient in the next bed called out to me, "Doctor, doctor". I went to him and explained that I was not a doctor. He replied, "Well you ought to be, you are so sympathetic". It was the best compliment I have ever received.

I lived in the world of a wonderfully run hospital for five weeks. When Frank was taken in, there were no private beds available, so he was there as a National Health Service patient. Had he been a private patient the only difference would have been that he would have had a private room. The nursing could not have been better, kinder, or more sympathetic. There was no hope for him, but at least he was splendidly nursed.

After his death I took Esmé away for a holiday. We went to Frank's apartment in Antibes. I was Frank's sole executor and his residuary legatee. His apartment is delightfully situated on the main boulevard, which leads down from the central square to the sea. I was feeling very shaken and Esmé was far from well. Whilst we were there she had a heart attack. The heart specialist warned me that her heart was in poor condition.

In Antibes we decided that it was time for us to retire; so when I got back I took the first steps towards putting the Royal on the market.

CHAPTER XXIII

THE END OF A PARTNERSHIP

We returned to an exceptionally heavy conference season. Despite her delicate condition, nothing could persuade Esmé to take things easily. She resumed her work through the night helping the night staff to get the hotel back into good order for the morning. I realised that the only way to give her relief was to get her out of the business and the simplest way to do it was to sell.

As it turned out there was little difficulty in finding a purchaser. The hotel company that bought the hotel was well known to me and I was able to negotiate a contract of sale with the completion date fixed for the end of the season.

It was an enormous relief to Esmé but she feared the outcome for me. She knew that I was totally immersed in my busy hotel life and she wondered how I should be able to cope with the quieter life of retirement. There was no time for regrets. The hotel was full right up to the date of the handover. We continued our routine until the end.

The best time of the day for both of us was the evening when we dined together. Sometimes in our apartment at the top of the hotel, sometimes in the main restaurant and at the weekends in the Cavalier, a restaurant in the basement with dimmed lights, a pocket handkerchief of a dance floor, a good dance band and a night club atmosphere. Our favourite was the small Gourmet Restaurant, which was beautifully equipped, well served and kept open until 1 a.m.

When the time of completion came, the main wrench was the leaving of our friends among the staff. They were indeed our best friends. We believed at the time, that the company we sold to, would provide reliable and lasting employment for them. We did not foresee that it would be taken over by a larger company, with the consequence that our hotel would become a pawn in a financial game of chess.

We came home to Scalby in October. After Christmas, we left for an extended holiday in Antibes. There was nothing much to do there other than to enjoy the delightful winter climate, wander down the narrow streets, sit in the little sheltered squares and the gardens by the sea and stroll around the ramparts to the harbour, full of private yachts of every type and size.

We explored every corner and gradually developed a quiet and enjoyable life, lunching out every day and having our evening meal in the apartment. I did the shopping, which was second nature to me as I had done it all my working life. At Antibes I found it fascinating. The small French tradesmen seemed to me to be superior to the British.

We stayed in Antibes for four months, living a happy, quiet and uneventful existence; but one day Esmé had another heart attack when walking back to the apartment after lunch at Antoine's *bistro*. Suddenly, I noticed she was in distress. Fortunately, the heart specialists' consulting rooms were close by, and we just managed to get there. The doctor was alarmed; he called me into his room to show me the violent oscillation of her heart, recorded on one of his testing instruments. We had to stay for a further month under his care until Esmé was fit to travel home.

At home, we settled down to retirement. It distressed Esmé to walk up the stairs, so we decided to build bedrooms on the ground floor, so that we would be able to live on one level. We came to the decision in 1965 but it was the Spring of 1966 before the work was put in hand, and then it took approximately a year to complete.

I had another building project in view. For many years I had longed to have a walled garden. I had even considered moving house to get one, but we were too attached to our home. So the only way was to build a wall around our existing kitchen garden. It was sheltered from the East and sloped gently down to the South. I decided to build a wall on the North and the West sides, one hundred and ten yards long and twelve feet high. I built it together with John Wardle, the husband of our cook. It took us a year, during which time we laid forty one thousand bricks! John took the leading part. It leans a little in places, but it is a grand wall and has proved a great asset to the garden.

Whilst we were building the wall, Raymond Hopkins, our gardener, made his third attempt to establish an asparagus bed. As we had had two failures, I made a study of asparagus culture and wrote a thesis on it. Raymond made the bed on the lines laid down in my thesis. This time, he was successful and we now have a well established bed, which provides one of the highlights of the gardening year. It is one of my most prized possessions.

In 1967 I took Esmé for one of her routine consultations with the heart specialist. He was alarmed by the degree to which her condition had worsened. He prescribed three weeks in bed, and said she should scarcely move a finger. Esmé felt that she would not be able to rest quietly at home. She asked me to take her to Antibes, where she promised she would rest completely and let me look after her.

The doctor agreed, provided we took extreme care. We arrived safely and Esmé went to bed in our apartment and allowed me to look after her. I did all the domestic work and nursed her. It was one of the happiest times of my life. I had sufficient company amongst the shopkeepers: Monsieur Chastel, the butcher in the Rue Sade, the most skilful I have ever known (he was more like a dissecting surgeon than the usual retail butcher); the proprietor of the little wine shop close by the top of the covered market, where on my shopping rounds I would take a glass of chilled Roussillon wine, generally two glasses, for it was delicious; and in the narrow Rue Sade there was a picture framer, Madame Tarallo, who occasionally had pictures for sale. I bought several beautiful paintings from her and she became a friend.

The Antibes heart specialist lived close to our apartment. He came to see Esmé every day. He was pleased with her progress but it was four weeks before he allowed her to get up. Then we were able to stroll to Antoine's for lunch, and after, to sit in the *Place de Gaulle* enjoying the winter sun. Esmé loved Antibes. We were so peaceful there with nothing to disturb our happiness.

At the beginning of December, we both had the feeling that we should return home. We flew back. The worst part of the journey was the long trek at Heathrow from the plane to the luggage hall. It was almost too much for her.

At home, I was concerned with a gallery of paintings that I was giving to the town of Scarborough. Mervyn Edwards, the town librarian and art gallery director, had prepared a delightful gallery to hold them. I went to supervise the hanging of the paintings and to add three pieces of beautiful furniture to enhance the effect. Three days before Christmas the hanging was completed.

That evening Esmé and I were sitting at either side of the fire. I told her I was pleased with the gallery and that I would like to take her to see it on the following day. "I would enjoy that", she said. I was looking across at her, it was extraordinary how beautiful she was, her age had not detracted from her gentle distinction. Suddenly she straightened up in her chair, her eyes dilating. I leapt up and embraced her, she did not make a sound, she was dead in my arms.

I dedicated the gallery to her memory. It is a lovely gallery, an appropriate memorial to a lovely person.

A few days after her funeral my friend Ruszkowski, the painter, came to stay with me. I told him that the best of my life was over. He was indignant. "You must never say that", he said. "As long as you have life you must live it to the full. How do you know what life has in store for you?" He was right, but that is another story.

APPENDIX

THE CHEF'S RECIPE
on
HOW TO SMOKE SALMON

Only the best quality fresh run salmon should be smoked. It is not satisfactory to smoke very large old fish and fish that have been up from the sea for a long time. The best size of fish for smoking is from 12 to 16lb. in weight. The smoking chamber should be constructed so that the fish can be hung up by the tail end from rods at the top of the chamber (with the head end downwards). The floor of the chamber should be 5 ft. above the source of the smoke, so that the smoke is cool by the time it reaches the chamber. The stove should be suitable for burning sawdust slowly and afford a good control over the fire by means of dampers and flues. The smoke generated needs to be steady but not heavy. If the floor of the smoke chamber is 5 ft. above the source of the smoke the temperature will be about right.

Oak chips and sawdust are the best fuels with the addition of green juniper twigs, which impart a better flavour to the fish after smoking.

The fish should first be washed and then filletted leaving the outer skin on both sides. The flesh should then be thoroughly pricked.

The next operation is to dry pickle the sides previous to smoking. The pickle used is constituted as follows:—

To each 1lb. of filleted fish — 1 oz. of coarse salt.

To each 1 lb of salt — 1 coffee spoon of saltpetre and 2 coffee spoons of Demerara sugar.

That is to 16 lb. of filleted fish:—

1 lb. of salt,
1 coffee spoon of saltpetre,
2 coffee spoons of Demerara sugar.

The fish fillets are placed in a tray and the pickle is rubbed gently into the pricked flesh and left over it. The pickle brings the moisture out of the fish and every 8 hours this should be poured off the tray and additional pickle gently rubbed into the fish. The process is continued over a period of 48 hours. The pickling must be done in a cool place.

After pickling for 48 hours, drain for 6 hours by hanging on a hook. After which the sides are hung in the smoking chamber by the tail with the head end downward, and smoked until dry, which takes approximately 6 hours. The temperature of the smoke chamber should not exceed 84 degrees. A higher temperature will break up the texture of the fish, which would then be liable to flake away when touched.

When the fish is taken out of the chamber and still warm it should be rubbed with olive oil and after stored in a cool place.

I have used the foregoing recipe for a number of years to smoke both salmon and sea trout with consistent success. It is important not to use too much pickle and to handle it gently. I obtain the oak shavings and oak sawdust from a local undertaker.

INDEX